Pray
and Play

Pray and Play

*101 creative prayer ideas
for use with under-fives*

Kathy Cannon

Scripture Union

To Grandma – my favourite Sunday School teacher
and Sophia Terry, for teaching me to pray and play.

A note on music
JP   *Junior Praise*, Marshall Pickering
ks   *kidsource*, Kevin Mayhew

Scripture Union, 207–209 Queensway, Bletchley, MK2 2EB, England.

Scripture Union is an international Christian charity working with churches in more than 130 countries providing resources to bring the good news about Jesus Christ to children, young people and families – and to encourage them to develop spiritually through the Bible and prayer.

As well as a network of volunteers, staff and associates who run holidays, church-based events and school Christian groups, Scripture Union produces a wide range of publications and supports those who use the resources through training programmes.

Email: info@scriptureunion.org.uk
Website: www.scriptureunion.org.uk

ISBN 1 85999 600 0

British Library Cataloguing-in-Publication Data
A catalogue record for this book is available from the British Library.

Cover design: Mark Carpenter Design Consultants
Front cover photographs: Steve Shipman
Back cover photograph: Edward Maas
Illustrations: Eira Reeves
Internal design: Carsten Lorenz
Cover printed: Ebenezer Baylis and Son Ltd
Internal pages printed and bound: Interprint, Malta

Contents

Introduction 7

Prayers

1.   ABC prayers 11
2.   Angels 11
3.   Animals, animals, animals . .12
4.   Animal masks 13
5.   Anyone thirsty? 14
6.   Baa, baa 14
7.   Baby, baby 15
8.   Badge-making 15
9.   Balloons 16
10. Balls in baskets 17
11. Banners, singing and praise .17
12. Bedtime 18
13. Birds 19
14. Birthdays 20
15. Bread 20
16. Bubble, bubble, bubble 21
17. Button boxes 21
18. Christmas 22
19. Circle of hands 22
20. Clean hands 23
21. Coat of many colours 25
22. Colours and objects 25
23. Computers 26
24. Creating creation 27
25. Creepy-crawlies 28
26. Easter eggs 29
27. Festival of Shelters 29
28. Finger puppets 30
29. Fishing 30
30. Fishy fish 31
31. Flower decorations 33
32. Food collages 33
33. Footprints 34
34. Forgetting 35
35. Friendship bracelets 35
36. Fun with fruit 36

37. Fun with play dough 37
38. Games 37
39. Glasses 38
40. Go, go, go! 39
41. God keeps his promises 39
42. God loves me 40
43. God's special box 41
44. Good food 42
45. Growing seeds 42
46. Having fun together 43
47. Hearts 44
48. I can help 45
49. Leaves 45
50. Lego homes 46
51. Let light shine 46
52. Long-jump praying 47
53. Making people welcome 48
54. Megaphone prayers 49
55. Mixed feelings 50
56. Mobile families 51
57. Model churches 52
58. Mountains and hills 52
59. Moving about 53
60. Moving house 53
61. Musical praise 54
62. Noah's ark 55
63. Paper chains 56
64. Paper people 57
65. Pass the parcel 57
66. Pavement prayers 58
67. Pet blessings 59
68. Picnic walk 59
69. Picture frames 60
70. Place mats 61
71. Play money 61
72. Please and thank you 62
73. Praising 62
74. Prayer cube 64

75.   Prayer wheels 64
76.   Pretty faces 66
77.   Puzzles 67
78.   Rainbow prayers 67
79.   Sand jars 68
80.   Sea creatures 70
81.   Sea shells 70
82.   Shapes 71
83.   Shopping 71
84.   Silent prayers 72
85.   Sky 72
86.   Stained-glass windows 74
87.   Story time 74
88.   Surprises 75
89.   Telephones 75
90.   Toy box 76
91.   Traceable bodies 77
92.   Uniforms 78
93.   Wakey, wakey 78
94.   Walls of Jericho 79
95.   Walking in the sand 79
96.   Watch a clock 80

97.   We are family 81
98.   Weather prayers 82
99.   Weddings 82
100. Wet feet 83
101. When I hurt myself 84

Training feature:
Play with a purpose 85

Appendix A:
Stocking a supply cupboard 89

Appendix B:
Bible references and related prayer
activities 89

Appendix C:
Bible topics and related prayer
activities 91

Appendix D:
Subject index 93

Introduction

Praying with children

Why pray with under-fives?

It's Sunday morning and an all-age service. In the front row, the children, even the toddlers, do the actions; they know all the words. The song finishes and a leader stands to pray. The children smile as they fold their hands and lower their heads. After a few moments and a long pause from the leader, one child shouts, 'Amen!' The congregation laughs.

But, one wonders, why pray with under-fives? Can they enjoy a relationship with God or should one wait until they're older to teach them about prayer? These questions are often asked in local churches and the answer will determine whether under-fives provision consists simply of a room full of toys or a more integrated programme of spiritual nurture.

We believe the Bible provides a clear mandate for passing on to and nurturing faith in small children – modelling and teaching prayer is a key part of that. In the Old Testament, for example, we read that parents were responsible for teaching God's instructions to their children within a family context (Deuteronomy 11:18–21). As they did so, God promised, '…your days and the days of your children [will] be many'. Likewise we see families in the New Testament bringing their children to Jesus.

> One day some parents brought their children to Jesus so he could touch them and bless them, but the disciples told them not to bother him. But when Jesus saw what was happening, he was very displeased with his disciples. He said to them, *'Let the children come to me. Don't stop them!* For the Kingdom of God belongs to such as these. I assure you, anyone who doesn't have their kind of faith will never get into the Kingdom of God.' Then he took the children into his arms and placed his hands on their heads and blessed them. (Mark 10:13–16, NLT, italics mine).

In the same way as adults had flocked to Jesus to be blessed and healed, children and babies were brought to him, too. It's clear from this passage that Jesus cares passionately for children, so much so that he rebuked the disciples for turning them away. Furthermore, Jesus uses the children as an example of the nature of faith to the families and disciples.

The aim of *Pray and Play* is to expose young children to faith and to encourage their spiritual growth as young children. These creative prayer ideas come from the understanding that pre-school children can experience God and have a relationship with him in their own right.

That relationship should always be appropriate to their age and development. Therefore, we want to create an atmosphere where we value and accept young children as Jesus did: welcoming them, wanting them and loving them for who they are *now* as well as who and what they may become. In the activities, we want to provide opportunities for young children to know and be known as individuals, whilst establishing an atmosphere of trust where they feel secure and can develop healthy self-esteem and confidence.

Pray and Play provides Bible-based, age-appropriate content that matches young children's needs and presents spiritual truths in ways that they can understand. (For a more detailed look at how to relate sharing faith to a child's stage of development, see *Children Finding Faith: Exploring a child's response to God* by Francis Bridger, SU, 1 85999 323 0). There is a variety of experiences and activities that are interesting, imaginative, enjoyable and stimulating, while running a God-thread throughout. It's important to acknowledge the different ways in which pre-school children learn and develop. So you'll notice that in these prayer ideas there's a lot of play, a key learning-model, and also a variety of ways to explore a theme, subject or truth.

All these elements help provide a framework of faith within which young children can build on their inherent spirituality and deepen their trust in God. Prayer is a vital part of that, both for adults and children.

In fact, the way in which we model prayer as adults will be very influential to a pre-school child. How can we show that talking to God is a vital part of our relationship with him? Many children observe that it is important to pray to God. We quite often encourage them to do so by folding their hands and saying a short prayer, usually before meals or bedtime. However, talking and listening to God is an integral part of the exciting business of being God's friend and getting to know him better, so we need to show that prayer can be fun and we can do it anywhere, anytime. We should also model the biblical pattern of needing and receiving prayer from our Christian family. It's an exciting challenge to think about how we can make our families households of faith where we talk to God together about our practical needs.

Practical tips for praying with under-fives

When using the ideas in *Pray and Play* to teach and model prayer, there are a few principles you may find helpful:

• Be imaginative. Some prayers may seem better suited to a group; yet all prayers can be used with as few as two people. Adapt as appropriate.

- Be relevant and flexible. Make sure you adapt activities to relate to the under-fives' environment, specific concerns, etc. Sometimes you will need to use the activities as general guides and not specific maps, depending on your circumstances.

- Communicate. Developing a child's relationship with God shouldn't be just a playtime activity. Families can share in the activities, relational emphasis and meaningful experiences. For a church, school, or other structured environment, you might consider sending a letter home with the child, explaining the prayer initiative and ways families can help.

- Evaluate. It is important to review regularly the impact of praying with children: how they've grown in their friendship with God and what spiritual areas still need nurturing. In doing so, one should be able to identify questions or misconceptions under-fives may have and lead them towards a more intimate relationship with God.

- Pray and play. Lastly and probably most importantly, those teaching and modelling prayer to children should have just as much fun playing and praying as those in their group. Prayer is a relationship of talking, listening and just spending time with your best friend, God.

It's not always possible to get children to be still or quiet. Fortunately, God loves prayers from the heart, no matter how they are delivered. The following are some helpful hints to consider depending on the type of *Pray and Play* activity:

Quiet prayers

- Encourage children to fold their hands if they're sitting still. This will prevent them from poking friends or playing.

- Children may close their eyes when praying. This should encourage them to focus on God and listening. However, children can also pray with their eyes open while focusing on a central picture or object related to God and prayer.

- Under-fives can hold hands with each other. Small children need physical contact. It's a vital factor in healthy child development, but in this day and age leaders of children's groups are aware that this can be fraught with difficulties. Encouraging children to hold hands with each other can be an important way of establishing 'safe' touch for them. There is also something very powerful about physical contact, even if it's simply a hand on the shoulder, when praying for each other as part of a community of faith.

- Create an atmosphere that encourages stillness. Cushions and music will help create a quiet environment to listen to God.

- Children can learn short, set prayers or phrases to repeat during a prayer time. This will provide them with a sense of accomplishment and a prayer they can learn and share with God anywhere.

- Quieter songs or rhymes with or without actions are another positive way to teach children a prayer they will remember.

- Children are very perceptive and imaginative about prayer needs. Ask them what they would like to pray for and about. Be sure either to incorporate their ideas into your prayer or encourage them to repeat their prayer requests after you.

- After praying, particularly with requests, leave space to listen to God, possibly with quiet music playing, before the 'close' of a prayer activity.

Active prayers

Moving prayers are just as valid and important as sitting still ones. God is listening no matter what we are doing. Active prayers model the fact that we can talk to God anywhere and anytime and not just at church or bedtime.

- Children sit still, but they also dance, sing, jog, and wriggle and these prayer positions are just as special to Jesus as the quieter ones.

- We all learn and retain more from doing than from just listening. A child will learn more about prayer and being God's friend by doing it than from just hearing about it.

- Prayer positions and actions can help explain the prayer. For example, children may hold their hands palms down. They can 'give' to God all the wrong things they've done or their fears. Afterwards, they can lift their palms upwards to receive God's forgiveness, love and peace. Alternatively, they can hold their hands up in the air, as a sign of wanting to receive from God or praising God. Actions in songs and rhymes are a method of saying and doing the prayer, making it easier for under-fives to learn.

- Dancing and songs are ways of praising God through prayer as well as singing words of repentance and thanksgiving.

- Dramas and role-play enable children to understand a specific character or emotion and are an excellent model for learning to pray and to be in relationship with God.

Listening to God

After praying, remind under-fives that we also need to listen to God. Talking is only one aspect of prayer – the other key element is listening. Prayer is part of a friendship with God and we need to give God time to talk back to us. So how can we help under-fives learn to hear God's voice?

- Encourage your pre-schoolers to learn Bible verses through rhymes and songs. God often brings his word to mind and uses it to speak to us, both at the time we learn it and also years later. Many adults find that verses they tucked into their memory banks as children are the ones that return when they need them later in life.

- Under-fives can draw pictures of Bible stories or a host of ideas from their imagination. Look at the pictures and talk about them with the child. God may use these to spark something to pray with the child about.

- As adults, we can ask God to be present in our everyday chat with small children or perhaps when we're trying to explain something difficult. We can trust him to use our words to say something to a child's heart without us even knowing.

These quiet, active and listening prayer ideas are just some of the ways we can model prayer and friendship with God. Trust God that as you work with under-fives, he will give you the confidence and creativity to create a secure playing environment where children can grow in faith, prayer and relationship.

When Jesus met the little children in Mark 10, we do not know the words they shared, the blessings Jesus gave, or how being in Jesus' presence changed those children's lives. However, we know an encounter with the living God can be life changing, no matter what our age. As members of God's family, let us encourage under-fives and children of all ages to come to God through praying and playing with their best friend, Jesus, and with their Christian church family. The effects of teaching the next generation to love chatting with God, wherever and whenever, are infinite.

Prayer activity sample page

You will need: Supplies are listed in order. Appendix A suggests basics for a craft cupboard. Where possible alternatives are given for unusual objects or toys.

Bible link

Topic   Verse

Where appropriate, a Bible reference or link that inspired or supports the prayer idea is included. A table at the back lists Bible passages and suggested prayer activities.

Preparation

Some prayer activities require adult preparation beforehand, depending on the age, size and maturity of the group. For instance, you could cut out pictures in advance if the children you work with are not very good with scissors yet. If you're working one-to-one, or with a small group, you may be able to do all the preparation with the children. For larger groups of children, it might be more convenient to accomplish as much as possible before they arrive.

Activity

This details what you and the children will need to do and includes comments and questions for the leader. Extend or curtail activities depending on your time limit and circumstances.

Prayer

There is a prayer at the end of each activity. You could use it or you may prefer to make up your own. Any special actions and instructions are in italics.

> **TOP TIP**
> Where appropriate, there are suggestions and further ideas which will add to the Pray and Play activity and theme.

Safety

Young children need constant supervision especially when using small items of equipment, and in particular when an activity involves water. Several of the activities in *Pray and Play* include cooking or using food. Always check beforehand with parents/carers about food allergies and whether or not children are permitted sweets and sugary drinks. It might be helpful to have a request for such information on the registration form, so that you can keep a record.

ABC prayer

(This activity can be done over several weeks.)

You will need: A5 card; thick marker pens; glitter and glue or glitter glue; medium-sized stickers; felt-tip pens or crayons; pencil.

Preparation

Choose up to four easily recognisable letters of the alphabet to write on the pieces of card, eg, a, b, c, d, p, s or t. Alternatively, write the first letter of each child's name. Outline each letter on the cards using pencil (for the children to trace) or a thick marker pen.

Activity

Show the children the cards and remark that they look very plain. Ask the children to decorate them. Be sure to put their names on the back before they begin so that you remember who did which. Provide them with an assortment of glitter, felt-tip pens and stickers. Alternatively, you can draw hollow letters and encourage the children to decorate the inside.

Collect up the decorated letters and show them to the children one by one, telling them the sound each letter makes. Think of a couple of words beginning with that sound before moving on to the next letter, get suggestions from the children. Make sure everyone who wants to has a turn. Note down any interesting suggestions for use in the prayer activity.

Prayer

Go through the alphabet cards. Either you or the children thank God for something beginning with that letter. Adapt the prayer below to suit your group's ideas.

Thank you God for aunties and apples.
Thank you God for babies and boys
Thank you God for cars and cuddles. Amen.

TOP TIP

Sing an alphabet song and have some free play with toy letters or alphabet puzzles. Look at alphabet picture books or play a simple 'I spy...' game, using letter-sounds not letter-names.

Angels

You will need: Christmas tree decorations and pictures depicting angels, eg, illustrations in a children's Bible, or Christmas cards; large circles (up to 1 m in diameter) or long rectangles (1 m by ½ m) of material or crêpe paper; silver or gold tinsel; sticky tape; glitter face paints (optional).

Bible link

God will put his angels in charge of you to protect you wherever you go: Psalm 91:11 (GNB).

Preparation

Find a good selection of angel pictures – see suggestions above. To make a circular cape or a long tabard, cut a hole in the circles or a slit halfway along the rectangles for the children to put their heads through. Make belts for the tabard out of tinsel.

Activity

Show the children the pictures of angels and the angel Christmas tree decorations. Ask what the angels are and what they do. Remind children that we don't really know what angels look like but we know God sends angels to look after us. The pictures are just ideas. Talk about the differences and similarities between the angels in the pictures.

In lots of the pictures, angels have beautiful bright clothes so tell the children that they're going to dress up in some lovely outfits. Dress the children in the capes or tabards. To make haloes, measure their heads with the tinsel, cut it and tape the cut ends together. If you wish, add some glitter face paint. Allow children some time to play. Encourage them to practise leaping and twirling.

Prayer

Invite them to twirl as everyone prays. Repeat a couple of times.

Thank you God for angels.
They are very special.
Amen.

Animals, animals, animals

You will need: Pictures of animals; toy animals; scissors; pen; basket.

Preparation

Select either some pictures of a variety of animals or use an animal picture-book. Try to find different animals for each letter of the alphabet. Hide the toy animals in a basket.

Activity

Ask the children if they've ever been to a zoo. Encourage them to talk about the trip and the animals they saw. Show them the pictures and allow them time to select their favourites.

Take the toy animals out of the basket one at a time. Encourage the children to have fun making noises and doing actions for each animal, such as hopping, galloping, digging, slithering, jumping, swimming, etc. Allow them some free time to play with the animals.

Prayer

Explain that you're going to say a little prayer, thanking God for animals. You will say 'Thank you God for (insert name of animal you have talked about or use the list below)' and that they can repeat after you, 'Thank you God for animals.'

Thank you God for the: *buzzing bee*
jumping jaguars
kicking kangaroos
loud lions
nibbling nanny goats
romping rabbits
slithery snakes
tough turtles.

Thank you God for animals.

Amen.

TOP TIP
Enjoy a trip to a children's zoo or an open farm.

Animal masks

You will need: *Large paper plates; scissors; hole punch; elastic; felt-tip pens or crayons; wool; glue or glue sticks; paint and paintbrushes; extra card.*

Preparation

Choose an animal for the masks to represent, eg a lion, bear or elephant. Punch a hole each side of the paper plate (for the elastic). Cut any extra pieces needed from the card, eg, small ears for a bear, big ears and a long trunk for an elephant. For a lion, cut strips of orange, yellow or brown wool to stick round the edge of the plate for the lion's mane. Finish one mask completely by painting or colouring the plate, attaching the elastic and extra pieces so that you have one to show the group. This mask should go on top of the head, rather than over the face, as young children often dislike having their faces covered.

Activity

Show the children your demonstration mask, linking it, if you wish, with an animal story or theme. Tell the children they can make masks too and give each a (named) paper plate, any other pieces plus glue and felt-tip pens. Help them colour and decorate their masks before adding elastic and knotting it so that it fits the child.

Let the children pretend to be the animals their masks represent, making animal noises and moving around like the animal.

Prayer

Invite the children to make an appropriate noise when you mention their animal.

Dear God, thank you for (name animal) and thank you for (name another animal),
And for the other amazing creatures in your world.
Thank you for making them all. Amen.

Anyone thirsty? (Aerobics)

You will need: Two jugs; water; squash; sparkling water; plastic cups.

Preparation

Fill one jug with water and make up the squash in the other. Place all the drinks and plastic cups out of the children's reach. Have a variety of exercises planned. Use the ones suggested below or your own but start slowly, warm up, stretch and cool down.

Activity

Welcome the children and say you're going to do some stretching and exercises. Invite them to join in. Begin with touching toes and stretching. Practise twisting side to side. Walk on the spot for a while and then step side to side.

Next, walk round the room. Do a few hops and jumps, a little jog and then a big run to the other end of the room. Ask if they're tired. If not, do a little more jogging and jumping. Once the children are tired, do a few, cool-down stretches, by repeating steps in reverse.

Ask who enjoyed that and whether exercising made them thirsty. Ask them what their favourite drink is. Explain that you have a few drinks they can try. Let them try water, then diluted squash and lastly, sparkling water. Make sure you open the sparkling water with the children, so they can hear the fizz.

Prayer

Invite the children to join in with some small actions for the prayer. Explain that when you say 'water', they can hold up their empty cups to God. When you say 'drink', they can either say 'gulp, gulp' or make gulping noises.

Dear God, we thank you for water (Hold up cups.)
and all we have to drink. (Make gulping sounds.) *Amen.*

Safety tip

Check with parents or carers before offering children anything but water to drink: even sparkling water can be harmful to teeth!

Baa, baa

You will need: Picture of sheep; paper plates; hole punch; picture of a sheep; cotton wool balls; glue sticks; paper ribbon or elastic; scissors.

Bible links

David the shepherd: 1 Samuel 16:11

The Lord is my shepherd: Psalm 23

We are God's sheep: Psalm 95:7

Jesus is the Good Shepherd: John 10:1–18

Preparation

To make sheep, punch two holes on either side of each plate.

Activity

Show the children a picture of a sheep. Ask them what sounds a sheep makes. Give them time to practise. Help them make their own sheep hats by gluing the cotton wool onto the plates. Attach paper ribbon or elastic to the paper plate and encourage the children to wear their sheep hats, like bonnets, fastened under their chins.

Gather the 'sheep' together and explain you're going to pretend to be a shepherd – someone who takes care of sheep. You're going to help all the sheep on the journey to a big field with lots of grass to nibble.

First go up the hill, walking very slowly. *(Huff and puff.)* Spot the goats. Run. *(Stop and pant.)* Have a nice lunch of grass *(Munch, munch.)* and a little afternoon sleep. *(Nap.)* When you wake up, you only have to go back down the other side of the mountain watching for the thorns in the bushes. *(Tiptoe.)*

Remind the children that just as a shepherd takes care of sheep, God takes care of us.

Prayer

Invite the children to say 'baa, baa' every time you say 'sheep'.

Dear God, thank you for fuzzy sheep (Baa, baa.)
and for shepherds who take care of sheep (Baa, baa.)
and thank you for taking care of us. Amen.

> **TOP TIP**
> When you finish your journey, have fun playing 'round up the sheep'.

Baby, baby

You will need: Baby dolls; blankets; nappies; pretend baby food (or empty plastic containers); plastic spoons; bottles; cribs/sleeping baskets.

Preparation

Put all the baby items into a basket or bag, which you can keep near you as you lead.

Activity

Talk to the children about babies. Allow them time to tell everyone about the babies they know.

Invite them to tell you what babies can and can't do, and show them the different baby items from your bag or basket that relate to their answers. Remind them that babies need a lot of care and that we must be gentle with them.

Show the children the baby dolls. Encourage them to take turns playing with the dolls, sharing some of the baby care items. When it is time to put the babies to bed, invite them to sing 'Rock-a-Bye Baby' and 'Hush Little Baby'.

Prayer

Let the children each hold a doll, as they pray. Explain they can hold their baby like you and copy your actions as you pray.

Dear Jesus, thank you for babies (Stroke the baby's head.) *and that we can help take care of them.* (Rock the baby.) *Amen.*

TOP TIP

You can use this story to introduce babies in the Bible such as Isaac (Genesis 21), Samuel (1 Samuel 1), Moses (Exodus 2:1–10) and Jesus (Matthew 1:18–25 and Luke 2:1–20).

Badge-making

You will need: A picture of each child (requested well in advance from parents and carers) or a Polaroid camera; A6 card; coloured markers, felt-tip pens or crayons; work badge (optional); glue sticks; glitter; small stickers; small safety pins; sticky tape.

Preparation

Well in advance, ask the children to bring in a photograph of themselves. Alternatively, use a Polaroid camera to take their pictures on the day. If you have a large group and a steady attendance pattern, write names on pieces of A6 card before they arrive – in marker or, for those old enough to trace, in pencil. You could also research what a child's name means and write it on the card. (A baby name book or baby websites such as www.babynamer.com are good resources.)

Activity

Tell the children that names are special to God. Jesus' name means 'the Lord saves'. Explain that when we were born, our families gave us names which have special meanings, too. If you have researched their names, tell the children what their names mean.

Explain that when some grown-ups go to work, they wear a special badge with their name and picture (if you have an example, show it to the group). This helps everyone to know each other's names. To help us remember each other's names, we're going to make our own name badges.

Let them glue their photo onto the card. Invite the older ones to trace the letters of their names. As you go around, remind the children what their names mean. Allow the children time to decorate their name badges with glitter and a few small stickers. Finally, secure the safety pin to the back of the card with the sticky tape. Then get the children into a circle and explain that you're going to practise saying everyone's names. Let each child stand in the centre and say their name. Invite the group to say, 'Hello, (child's name)'. If you are using this activity with a very small group, you could make badges for other siblings, family members, dolls and teddy bears.

Prayer

Remind the children that are we are special to God and he knows each one of our names.

Sing 'I'm special because God has loved me' (JP 106) or pray:

Thank you God that you know all our names and you love us. Amen.

Balloons

You will need: *Balloons (assorted colours); baskets (optional).*

Preparation

Blow up the balloons, at least one per child, and scatter them around the room.

Activity

Welcome the children and point out that there are balloons everywhere. Ask them to help you collect them and put them in one pile. Once you've gathered them all together, talk about what the children like doing with balloons. Try out some of their suggestions for a few minutes, throwing, catching, keeping the balloons off the floor and rubbing balloons on their hair and making them stick to their stomachs or the walls.

Scatter the balloons and ask the children to collect them once more. Next, talk about the colours of the balloons. Encourage them to say the colours with you and to sort the balloons into piles or baskets by colour. Invite the children to choose a balloon each and make a circle to pray. Let them take their balloons home with them.

Prayer

Explain to the children that it's good to say thank you to God for things like balloons.

Invite them to hold their balloons up when you thank God for that colour and then everyone can hold up their balloons when you say, 'Amen'.

Dear God, we thank you for red balloons,
   (Hold up red balloons.)
and thank you for blue balloons,
   (Hold up blue balloons.)
and thank you for green balloons.
   (Hold up green balloons.)
God, thank you for all the fun we have with balloons.
   (Everyone hold up balloons.)
Amen.

Balls in baskets

You will need: *Balls or beanbags of different sizes and colours (at least three per child); baskets and/or boxes; sticky tape or string.*

Preparation

Arrange baskets and/or boxes of various sizes and shapes around the room, placing some on the ground and some a bit higher, eg, on a chair, held securely by tape or string. Place all the balls or beanbags in one central basket.

Activity

Invite the children to join you for an exploration of the room. Show them the balls or beanbags in the centre basket and all the boxes and baskets around the room. As a practice, give each child a ball from the centre basket and encourage them to put it in any basket around the room. Then, ask them to collect a ball from a different basket and put it back in the central basket. Explain that in a minute, you're going to empty the whole basket of balls on the floor for the children to collect and put into baskets.

Gather the children to a starting point, where they must wait until you say, 'Go!' (You don't want them tripping over moving balls.) Tip all the balls onto the floor. When they stop rolling, encourage the children to pick one up and put it in a basket. Continue until all the balls are picked up. Then add a challenge by bringing a few baskets closer to you. Designate particular baskets for different colours or types of ball and encourage them to repeat the activity, this time putting the balls of the same size or colour together.

Prayer

Let each child hold a small ball. Place a basket in the centre of the prayer circle. When you say 'Amen', let them throw their balls in the basket.

Thank you God for playing and balls. Amen.

Banners, singing and praise

You will need: *A5 pieces of paper; glue sticks; drinking straws; marker pens; Christian music suitable for children; CD/cassette-player.*

Preparation

To make a flag, fold the A5 paper in half, short sides together. Put glue on one inner half of the card. Insert the straw on the folded edge and press the top half of the card onto the glued bottom half of the card.

Write 'Praise God' on the flag.

Bible link

We will shout for joy ... lift up our banners: Psalm 20:5

Activity

Ask who likes to sing. After hearing a few answers, ask the children if they think God likes us to sing. Affirm that God loves to hear us sing, especially when we sing songs for him. There is a special word in the Bible – hallelujah. Get them to say the word with you. Explain that it means 'Praise God, everybody!' Sometimes, when people sing, they like to wave banners and flags and dance, too.

Give them a ready-made flag, or encourage them to follow the preparation steps to make their own. Wave the flags, reminding them to be careful not to hit anyone. Practise a little side-stepping or wiggling dance. Explain that you're going to sing or play some music that says how wonderful God is. Encourage them to sing and either wave their flags or dance. (See Top tip overleaf for song suggestions.) To prevent injury, don't let them wave flags and dance at the same time. Play the music and let the praising begin. Don't forget to join in yourself because you're the best example!

Prayer

Teach the children to mime the words as they do the actions.

We can sing. (Shout '*sing*'.)
We can praise. (Wriggle.)
We can wave our flags to you. (Wave flag.) *Amen.*

TOP TIP

Try 'If you're happy and you know it', using the words, 'wave your flag… stamp your feet… shout Amen.' *Let's Sing and Shout!* and *Let's all clap hands!* edited by Maggie Barfield (SU) contain lots of praise songs and rhymes you can use. For Christian praise music, try *Great Big God* (Vineyard Music, UK).

Bedtime

You will need: *Sleeping mats; blankets and pillows/cushions; toothbrush (optional); bedtime stories; soft/cuddly toys.*

Activity

Explain to the children that you're pretending it's nighttime and you're tired. Talk together about what they do when they go to bed. Ask them to help you get ready for bed. Let them tell you what you need for bedtime. When they say 'a bed', ask them to help you set up the sleeping mats as beds. Ask if they need anything else to keep them warm and comfortable. Offer blankets and pillows.

Ask if they can get into bed now. Remind them to brush their teeth. They may suggest a drink. If so, mime drinking a glass of milk or water. Make sure it's 'just a quick one'. Is there anything else? Remind them about their cuddly toys to keep them company.

Once they're in bed, ask if they'd like to hear a bedtime story. Read *Good Night, Spot* by Eric Hill (Frederick Warne) or something similar. Close quietly with the prayer below. Encourage them to repeat it with you. Pretend to sleep, then wake up with a shout, 'Amen!' Encourage them to join you in shouting, 'Amen!'

Prayer

Explain that you're going to teach them a short prayer to say before they go to bed.

Good night, (Blow a kiss.)
God bless. (Blow a kiss.)
See you in the morning! (Blow a kiss.)

Birds

You will need: Coloured material or paper; scissors; orange card cut into squares approximately 7.5 cm x 7.5 cm; sticky tape; elastic; hole punch; bread; napkins; pictures of birds.

Preparation

You are going to dress the children as birds. Using the coloured material or paper, cut out circular capes (up to one metre in diameter) with holes for heads. The children may need to share.

To make beaks, cut the orange squares diagonally into two triangular pieces. Fold each in half and open up again. Lay one triangle on top of the other and tape them together at each of the two corners on the long side of the triangle (see diagram). When you hold these corners and push in, the beak will open. Punch holes near these two corners and insert a piece of elastic on either side to fit round a child's head. Make enough beaks for everyone or just enough for those with capes to alternate with those with beaks. Break the bread into small pieces and place on the napkins.

Activity

Ask the children where they get their food. Talk about their answers. Show the pictures of birds and ask what birds they've seen and what sounds the birds make. Practise bird noises! Then ask what birds eat and how they get their food. Explain that birds like seeds, grass and bread.

Talk about how birds move by flapping their wings very fast. Explain that people can't fly like birds, but we can move our arms very fast. Enjoy a practice, pretend flight.

Put the napkins with the bread pieces around the room so that the birds can eat. Give each of the children a cape and/or a beak. Let them be birds who chirp, fly with their cape 'wings' and eat bread.

Prayer

Invite the children to 'coo, coo' and flap their 'wings' like a bird every time you say 'bird'.

Dear God, we thank you for birds (Coo, coo.)
and that birds (Coo, coo.) can find bread to eat. Amen.

TOP TIP

This is an ideal introduction to Elijah: tell the story of how the birds shared their food with him (1 Kings 17:1–6).

Birthdays

You will need: Icing; child-friendly spatulas or knives; balloons; birthday plates and tablecloth; small cupcakes or tea cakes (remember to check for children's allergies); sprinkles; edible cake decorations or sweets; candles (optional); party bags with a few treats or sweets; cling film.

Preparation

Place the icing in small bowls with child-friendly spatulas or knives and cover with cling film.

Blow up the balloons.

Activity

Talk to the children about birthdays and parties. Let them share their experiences.

Show them the birthday plates and tablecloth and invite them to a pretend birthday party. Let them help set the table, then sit everyone down. Give each child a cake and get them to decorate it with the icing, sprinkles and sweets before eating (remember health and hygiene regulations). Depending on the group size and age, you could let children blow out a candle one at a time before eating their cakes. Let them enjoy the party balloons and bags.

Prayer

Invite the children to help you tidy up. As they do, help them to say:

Thank you God for parties. Amen.

> ### TOP TIP
> Sing 'Happy Birthday'. Insert 'us' and 'everyone' instead of 'you' and a name.

Bread

You will need: Bread dough; flour; decorations such as raisins, choc chips or sunflower seeds, etc; baking trays; towel; handwashing facilities; greaseproof paper; aprons; floor covering; oven.

Bible links

Jesus feeds the five thousand: Matthew 14:13–21; Mark 6:30–44; Luke 9:10–17; John 6:1–15

The Last Supper: Matthew 26:17–30; Mark 14:12–26; Luke 22:14–23

The Lord's Supper: 1 Corinthians 11:17–34

Preparation

Beforehand, make enough dough for the whole group. Remember to check carefully for allergies with the dough and anything else that the children will add. Also make some different shapes with extra dough, a turtle with little balls for feet, a snake, a cottage loaf, etc. Preheat the oven, cover the floor and set out the other items.

Activity

Show the children the dough and explain that today you're going to make bread shapes together. Get them to wash their hands and put on aprons. If you have a large group, divide into smaller groups, each with an assistant. Remember health and hygiene rules.

Give each child a piece of dough. Let them practise rolling and kneading it. Show them the items you made and give them time to shape their own dough, adding raisins, etc as eyes, spots or other decorations.

Place their creations on the baking trays on a piece of greaseproof paper with the child's name and put in the oven. Keep children away from oven. While the bread is baking, read a story about Jesus feeding the five thousand, such as *Share out the Food with Jesus – an Action Rhyme book* by Stephanie Jeffs and Chris Saunderson (SU). Take the bread out of the oven and leave to cool. Pray and then enjoy it together.

Prayer

Thank you God for bread and the shapes we've made. Amen.

> ### TOP TIP
> You could explain to your group that Jesus had a special meal with his disciples where they ate bread and drank special grape juice called wine.

Bubble, bubble, bubble

You will need: *Pots of bubble mixture or washing-up liquid and small containers such as yoghurt pots; bubble wands (can usually be bought in a multi-pack).*

Preparation

Make bubble mixture using one part washing-up liquid to ten parts water, then divide into small containers. Alternatively, buy pots of bubbles. Children may find it easier if you put the bubble-mix containers on a low table.

Activity

Ask the children if they like bubbles. Ask what we do with them. Blow a few bubbles and encourage the children to run and pop them. Allocate the bubble pots and wands and give children time to blow bubbles. Then see who can blow a small bubble, the biggest bubble, the most bubbles…

Prayer

To close, explain that in a moment, everyone will blow some bubbles. Then, as they float, everyone can say a quiet prayer to God. When the last bubble pops, everyone can shout 'Amen.'

Dear God, thank you for bubbles. (Blow bubbles then leave space for silent prayers.) *Amen.*

Button boxes

You will need: *Small boxes; scissors; assortment of buttons; items of clothing with different ways of fastening; glue sticks; stickers; glitter; felt-tip pens or crayons.*

Preparation

Lay out the items, ready to make button-lid boxes.

Activity

Ask the children if they know what buttons are. Encourage them to point to any on their clothes.

What are buttons for? They fasten our clothes. Show items with zips or other fasteners and explain that they do the same job as buttons.

Show the children some loose buttons – ideally ones with interesting textures. Let them handle them. Encourage some sorting activities, eg sorting by colour and size. Ask the children if they'd like to make a box with a button lid. Invite everyone to sit at a table and encourage the children to choose a few to glue to their box lid. They may also want to place a few buttons inside their boxes. Let them decorate the boxes, too.

Prayer

Invite the children to do the actions with you, as you pray.

Dear God, thank you for big things like us,
   (Hold arms out wide.)
and little things like buttons.
   (Hold thumb and first finger together in a circle.)
Thank you for our boxes,
   (Point to their boxes.)
and the fun we've had making them.
   (Make a smiling face with hands.)
Amen.

Safety note

Attempt this activity ONLY with 4 and 5 year-olds and with plenty of adult supervision. Young children will be tempted to put buttons in their mouths. For younger children substitute stickers for buttons.

Christmas

You will need: Christmas tree and stand; tinsel; plastic ornaments with large hooks; edible decorations (enough for one per child and suitable for children with allergies).

Preparation

Position the Christmas tree in the centre, so there is access all round. Secure the base, so that it doesn't fall over. Make sure the ornaments can be put on the tree with little fingers!

Activity

Ask the children if they know what special day is coming soon. Talk about what happens at Christmas. See who has a Christmas tree at home yet and if they helped decorate it.

Point to the bare tree and invite the children to help you decorate it. Remind them to be careful with the ornaments and tree. Only have a couple of children putting ornaments on at one time, in case the tree falls over.

Allow them time to decorate, add some tinsel and edible decorations/candy canes. When you have finished, admire the tree and let them talk about their own trees.

Prayer

Make a big circle around the tree and hold hands. Encourage the children to practise running in towards the tree (not too close) and back away from it. In a lively voice, sing the words below to the tune of 'Oh Christmas Tree'. Explain that for each line, they will run in, run back and then walk in and have a sweet. Repeat until all tree sweets are gone.

Oh Christmas Tree, (Run in towards the tree.)
Oh Christmas Tree, (Run back away from the tree.)
Thank you God for Christmas! (Walk in towards the tree and have a sweet.)

> ### TOP TIP
> Enjoy some Christmas songs like 'Frosty the Snowman' and 'Rudolph the Red-Nosed Reindeer'.

Circle of hands

You will need: Newspaper; one sheet of poster card; handwashing facilities; kitchen roll/towel; thick poster paint; large shallow bowls; aprons; A4 card (optional).

Preparation

Place newspaper on the floor and tables where the prayer activity will take place. Lay the poster card in the centre of the table. Prepare handwashing facilities nearby. Place the paint in the large shallow bowls next to the poster card.

Activity

Talk to the children about hands and fingers. Ask if they know any finger rhymes or songs and do some together ('Two Little Dicky Birds', 'This Little Piggy', etc). Let the children show you what else they can do with their hands and fingers and try some suggestions such as tickling or picking things up.

Remark that it's exciting to have hands and fingers because of all the things we can do with them. Say you're going to make a special poster with all your hand prints together. Explain that everyone will get a chance to dip one hand into the paint and then onto the poster. Make everyone put on an apron before you start.

To make the group poster, get each child in turn to put their hand into the paint and then onto the large sheet. When each child has placed their handprint, rotate the paper, so that all the fingers overlap slightly. When children have put their prints on the big poster, they could be given a piece of named A4 card to make a print to take home, before washing and drying their hands.

Show the finished poster to the children. Point out that all the fingers touch on the picture because you all belong together here. Find a special place to hang your poster.

Prayer

As you pray, explain that just as all the fingers touch on the poster, so you're all going to hold hands as we pray.

Thank you God for our fingers and all we can do with them – paint, eat, play and draw.
Thank you that we can be friends and hold hands, too.
Amen.

Clean hands

You will need: Newspaper; large bowl; water; compost; kitchen roll/towel; handwashing facilities.

Preparation

Place newspaper on the floor and under the tables where the prayer activity will take place. Fill the bowl with compost. Have the handwashing facilities nearby.

Activity

Ask the children if they have ever played outside and got really dirty? Allow them time to talk about it. Show them the compost and let them put their hands in, sift and feel it. (Some children get distressed at the thought of touching something dirty and will not want to do this activity. It's important not to force them but encourage adult carers to join in, modelling to the children that it's OK.)

If you have access to a safe, enclosed garden, you could do this activity outside with compost or sand. If you're happy for things to get a little messier and the children's clothes are well protected, add a little water and allow them to have fun with wet material. Talk about what it feels like.

To finish, ask what their parents/carers say when they are dirty and how they get clean. Remove the compost. Explain that it's very important to wash our hands when we've been playing with anything messy. Wash and dry hands.

Prayer

Invite them to wiggle their fingers as you pray.

Thank you God that we can have fun playing with wet things and dry things and that we can clean our hands, too. Amen.

Safety note

Ordinary soil from your garden may contain harmful microbes. Sterilised compost is obtainable from most garden shops.

Coat of many colours

You will need: A4 pieces of card; scissors; scraps of material (assorted sizes, colours and textures); glue and spreaders or glue sticks; glitter; stickers; felt-tip pens or crayons.

Bible link

Joseph and his coat: Genesis 37

Preparation

Draw a simple, tunic-style, coat on each card – one for each child. If necessary, cut the material into small pieces that the children can glue easily.

Activity

Invite the children to bring their coats for a story about a boy named Joseph and his coat. Explain that Jacob, his dad, gave him a new coat. Let the children show you their coats and remind them that coats keep us warm. Tell them Joseph's coat had lots of colours on it; the colours made it look really nice. Point out the colours in the children's coats.

Show the children the material and the outlines on the cards. Allow them to feel the different textures and comment on the patterns and colours. Remind them that Joseph's coat was very colourful, like the scraps of material you have.

Help the children glue the scraps of material onto the outlines and decorate with glitter, felt-tip pens and stickers.

Remind the children that Joseph's daddy gave him his coat. Ask them where their clothes come from. Comment on the things the children are wearing. Help them identify tops, trousers, dresses, skirts, socks, shoes and coats. Remind them that their mummies and daddies/carers give them nice clothes too. Encourage them to thank God for people who take care of them and give them coats to keep them warm.

Prayer

Invite the children to join in the actions with you as you pray.

Dear God, thank you for warm coats to wear.
  (Hug yourself as you shiver.)
Thank you for the colourful coats we made.
  (Invite the children to hold them up.)
Thank you for people who take care of us.
  (Jump up.)
Amen.

Colours and objects

You will need: Basket; fruit or small sweets; assorted objects in different colours, such as card, felt-tip pens or crayons, pieces of material, large buttons, books, toothbrushes, paintbrushes, plastic cups, children's cutlery, soft toys.

Preparation

Select a variety of multiple objects in different colours – see list above. Place them in the basket.

Activity

Show the children your basket. Ask what they can see. Suggest they help you sort everything by colour. Let a few children select items of different colours. Say the name of the colour and let them make piles of different coloured objects. Encourage everyone to take at least one item from the basket and put it in a pile with similar colours.

Next, look at each pile, checking that all the items are the same colour. Point out that there are different shades of colours – such as bright and light colours.

If you have time for a further activity, explain to the children that you think you'll need their help again. Say that all the toothbrushes are in different piles, so are the buttons, the paintbrushes, the soft toys and so on. Ask the children to help you by making piles of similar things. Help them collect up all the paintbrushes, then buttons, etc and place them in new piles.

To finish, you could give everyone a colourful snack, such as pieces of fruit or coloured sweets, and point out the different colours.

Prayer

Invite each child to hold something they picked up.

Dear God, thank you for all the colours and all the different things we have. Amen.

Computers

This activity will work best in a small group so that all the children have the opportunity to have a go on the computer.

You will need: Children's and/or toy computers (also you could make some out of cardboard boxes with a sheet of paper stuck on to make a screen and a pretend keypad); a real computer with a keyboard and mouse; mouse mats.

Preparation

Place the toy computers around the room. Put the real computer, keyboard and mouse in a safe place, making sure the computer is turned on, any programs loaded and that it's ready to go.

Activity

Ask the children who's seen or played on a computer. You can find them in lots of places: a library, nursery school or perhaps they have one at home?

Point out the computers – both toy or real. Explain that everyone will have a turn to look at the real computer but while they're waiting they can play with the toy computers. Allow a few children at a time – with adult supervision – to look at the real computer and type gently on the keyboard. Use a child's CD-ROM or, if you have internet access, check out sites like www.bbc.co.uk/cbeebies.

Prayer

Set up a very simple template page and have a couple of images (ie clip art) ready. Let the children choose which pictures to put on the page. Type a simple 'thank you' prayer and print it off for them to take home.

TOP TIP

There are usually plenty of computer-literate folk around who are willing to lend their expertise in setting up a computer and printer for your session. Ask them to set up a simple document page and find some images for you.

Creating creation

You will need: Newspaper; small containers for paint; kitchen roll/towel; paint (yellow, brown, blue, green, white and red) and paintbrushes; A4 card in a neutral colour; aprons; handwashing facilities; blank sheet of paper.

Bible link

Creation: Genesis 1–2

Preparation

Place newspaper on the floor and tables where the prayer activity will take place. Fill small containers with paint and place on the table with the blank card and paintbrushes. Have one or two paintbrushes for each colour.

Activity

Make the children put on aprons to protect their clothes. Explain that you're going to tell a story and as you do, they can paint it on their cards. Encourage them to listen for the colours. Point out the different colours of the paint before you start. Keep the story moving quickly, as they may paint faster than you talk!

Show the children the blank sheet of paper. Explain that in the beginning everything was blank and plain. God decided to create lots of colourful things to put in the world. First, he added light and darkness. Then God made the sky. Ask the children what colour the sky is in the daytime and allow them to paint a blue sky.

Next, God added the land and sea. Invite the children to paint a brown strip across three quarters of the lower part of the card, filling in the rest with blue sea. But, the earth looked plain, so God created trees, plants, grass, and flowers. Allow them time to paint green vegetation above the brown strip.

Then, God created day and night. Paint a yellow sun and a white moon. Explain that it was quiet and ask what they think could make some noise? You could make some animal noises if they don't guess. Allow them time to paint some animals. Next, God created two people called Adam and Eve. Let the children draw people, then give them some time to finish their paintings. (Note – don't worry if the animals and people are unrecognisable!)

Finally, say that when God had finished making the world, he had a rest. While the pictures dry, wash everyone's hands and sing 'He's got the whole world in his hands' (JP 78) or 'Who's the king of the jungle?' (ks 388)

Prayer

Invite the children to hold up their pictures as they say together.

Thank you God for making our colourful world.
Thank you for yellow, blue, green and brown,
And thank you God for making me! Amen.

TOP TIP

Children will undoubtedly want to use the same colour paint at the same time, so if you have a large group, make sure that you provide lots of containers of the same colour so that a maximum of two share each colour.

Creepy-crawlies

You will need: Book about insects (suitable for young children); bug boxes; assortment of creepy-crawlies; kitchen roll.

Preparation

Using the bug boxes, collect an assortment of creepy-crawlies such as a worm, an ant, a ladybird, a spider, a wood-louse, etc. Put the bug boxes with their contents safely at the side of the room.

Activity

Ask the children if they like playing out of doors. Have they ever found any creepy-crawlies? Let them tell you about them.

Show them the book about insects. Let them point to the ones that they've seen. Explain that you have some creepy-crawlies to show them. Tell them that the creepy-crawlies must stay in the boxes and they can't touch them or they'll escape.

Show them what you have brought, telling the children their names and pointing out their different characteristics: number of legs, size, colour. Comment on how fast or slowly they move.

Stress that at the end of the session you are going to put them all back in the garden where you found them.

Put the bug boxes back in a safe place and invite the children to imitate the creepy-crawlies they've just been looking at. Encourage them to practise scrambling on the floor, pretending they have eight legs, wiggling like a worm, etc. Whilst doing this, let them sing any relevant songs such as 'Incy-wincy spider'.

To finish, read a story about creepy-crawlies such as *The Very Busy Spider* by Eric Carle (H Hamilton).

Prayer

Dear God, thank you for creepy-crawlies, and all the different things about them.

Thank you that I'm special too. Amen.

> ### TOP TIP
> Bug boxes are specially made boxes with magnifying glass, to enable close inspection of creepy-crawlies!

Easter eggs

(Use this activity a week or two before Easter)

You will need: *Hard-boiled eggs (2–3 per child); felt-tip pens; stickers; fabric scraps; glue sticks; handwashing facilities.*

Preparation

Prepare the hard-boiled eggs. It normally takes 7–10 minutes in boiling water. Set out the felt-tip pens and other decorations for the children to use.

Activity

Ask the children what special day will soon be here. Explain that you're going to decorate eggs for Easter. Help them decorate their Easter eggs by colouring them with felt-tip pens and sticking on other decorations.

Depending on the length of your session, you could have an egg hunt or egg and spoon race. (You could use this activity at other times in the year, focusing on the egg decorating, not on Easter.)

Close with an egg snack, possibly with crackers and toast, but always check for food allergies first!

Prayer

Invite the children to hold up their Easter egg when you say 'eggs' and 'Easter'.

Dear God, thank you for eggs and special times, like Easter. Amen.

> **TOP TIP**
> You could make enough Easter eggs for a special lunch or church event.

Festival of Shelters

You will need: *Easily erected 'tents' – these can be play tents or blankets draped over chairs; sleeping bags; camping mats; camping equipment such as picnic sets, torches and folding chairs.*

Bible link

The Festival of Shelters: Leviticus 23:33–44

Preparation

Set up all the tents in a large circle with their entrances facing inwards.

Activity

Ask if any of the children have been camping and let them talk about the experience. Discuss differences between their houses and camping. Point out that a tent doesn't have a bathroom, a kitchen or even beds – you sleep in sleeping bags.

Invite children to sit in and around the entrances to the tents. Tell the story of God's special people, the Israelites. When God rescued them from Egypt they had to live out of doors for a while until they could settle in their own land and could build real houses. When they were settled, God told them to celebrate a special feast. Every year, they took leafy branches and made tents outside. They lived out of doors in their tents for a whole week and had a lovely time, singing to God and praying, and remembering how he had looked after them long ago.

Prayer

Use the opportunity to sing a few songs and/or pray together.

Thank you God that you looked after your special people the Israelites. Thank you that you look after us too. Amen.

Finger puppets

You will need: *Large circles of card (one for each child); A4 sheets of thin card; crayons or paints; glue and spreaders.*

Preparation

Cut the A4 card into strips widthways about 3 cm wide.

Activity

Give each child a circle and strip of card and explain that they're going to make their own spiders and use their fingers as pretend legs for the spider. Get them to decorate their card with eyes and any other patterns. Attach the strip of card to the underside (the undecorated side) of the spider to act as a handle. Show the children how to put their four fingers through the handle so that the spider card is on the top of their hand. Practise 'walking' the spider along with your fingers and sing 'Incy-wincy spider' with actions.

Prayer

'Walk' your spiders into the middle of the group and say:

Thank you God for my wiggling fingers!

TOP TIP

You could adapt this idea to make a ladybird, grasshopper or any other kind of bug.

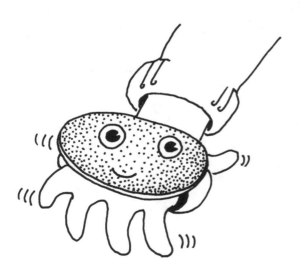

Fishing

You will need: *Small paddling pool (or several large bowls); newspaper; water; plastic fish (or waterproof objects like plastic bottle caps); sheet or cover for pool; two large towels; aprons.*

Bible links

Jesus calls the first disciples to be fishers of people: Mark 1:17

Jesus calls Simon Peter: Luke 5:4–11

Jesus appears to the disciples after his resurrection: John 21:1–14

Preparation

Place the pool on newspaper and add just enough water for the fish to float. Add the fish or other plastic toys and place a cover over it.

Activity

Tell your chosen story using a children's Bible or your own words. Below, you'll find the story for Simon Peter.

Simon Peter was a fisherman. (*Ask the children what fishermen do. Explain that they try to catch fish. Sometimes they stand on a pier and sometimes they go out in a boat. Invite the children to tell you how they think it feels to catch a fish. Exciting? What if they didn't catch a fish?*) One day, Jesus came and got into Simon Peter's fishing boat. After a little while, he told Simon to sail the boat out onto the lake and let down his nets to catch some fish. Simon Peter was very tired. 'Jesus,' he said, 'we've been out all night fishing but we haven't caught a single fish. But because you've asked me to, I'll try again.'

They sailed out into the deep water and let down their nets to see if they could catch some fish. What do you think happened when they tried to pull in their nets? They had caught so many fish that they had to call their friends to help them lift the nets out of the water. Their boats were full of the shiny, silvery fish as they sailed back to shore.

Simon Peter was astonished. He knew that Jesus must be a very special person to help them catch so many fish.

Ask the children if they'd like to practise fishing. Help them to roll up their sleeves and put on aprons. Remove the sheet/cover from the pool and let the children fish with their hands. When all the fish have been caught, you could throw them back in and try again. At the end, dry the children and the fish. Empty the water away.

Prayer

Let children hold their fish up.

Thank you Jesus for the pretend fish we caught and for the fun we've had! Amen.

TOP TIP

You can also have fun 'fishing' by making simple rods with thread or wool and a magnet and attaching paper clips to the fish.

Safety note

Remember that young children can drown in just a few centimetres of water. NEVER leave children unattended near water.

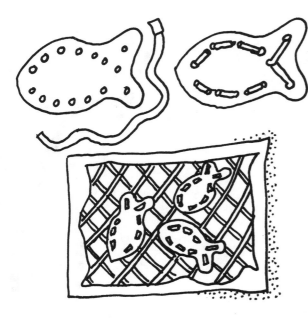

Fishy fish

You will need: *Coloured A4 card – one sheet per child; hole punch; coloured laces from an educational supplier or lengths of coloured wool with the ends sticky-taped to make them firm enough to push through holes; garden netting or length of blue fabric to display.*

Bible link

Jesus feeds the five thousand: Matthew 14:13–21; Mark 6:30–44; Luke 9:10–17; John 6:1–15

Preparation

Trace a simple fish shape onto the cards (template overleaf) and cut it out. Punch a series of holes round the edge of the fish. If using wool, cut into 50 cm lengths and tape the ends. If possible use different colours of card and wool. To make a 'demo' fish, sew the wool or lace through the holes in the fish outline.

Activity

Ask the children if they've ever seen a fish. Let them tell you about it. Show them how to make 'fish lips' – imitating fish by opening and closing their mouths – and let them practise. Ask where fish live. When you've established that it's in water, talk about water together – what does it feel like? What colour is the sea? Usually it looks blue.

Show the children the fish card you have laced previously and invite them to make one each too. Show them how to lace in and out of the holes. Put children's names on the back of the cards before they begin. (Enlist plenty of adult help as many small children get in a muddle about where the lace goes next!) When a child finishes, allow them to take the fish for a swim around the room. Mount the fish on garden netting or a piece of blue fabric.

To close, you could tell the story of the loaves and fishes.

Prayer

Invite the children to make 'fish lips' as you pray.

Thank you God for fish. Amen.

TOP TIP

This activity can be adapted to other themes by varying the objects on the lacing cards, eg, stars, hearts, flowers.

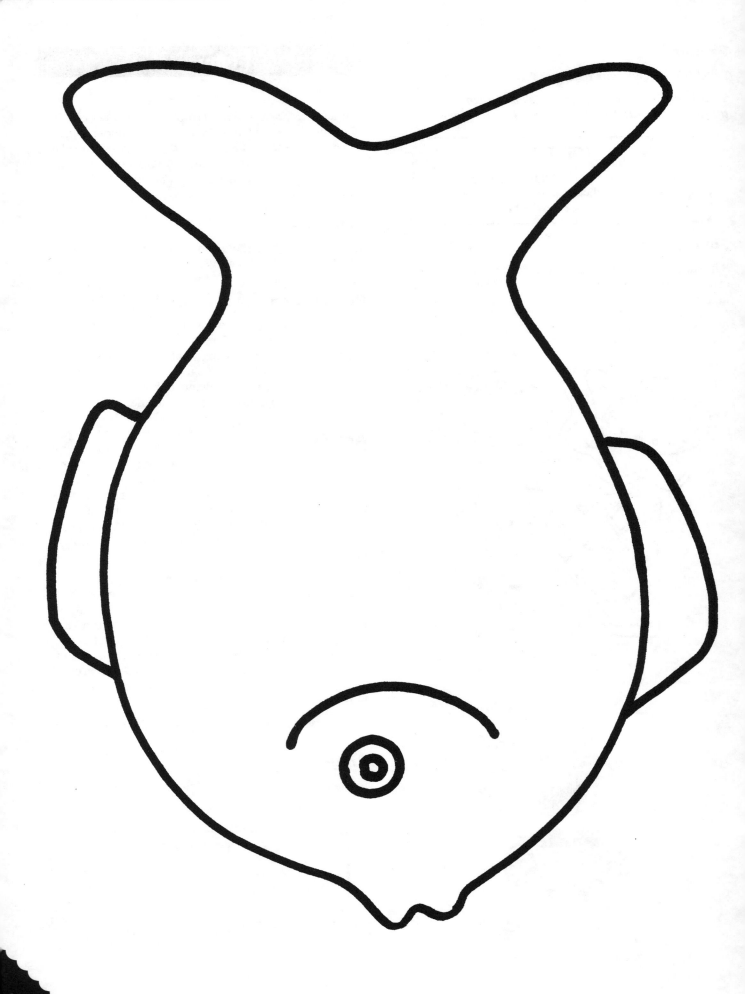

Flower decorations

You will need: Newspaper; OASIS® floral foam; large bowl; water; flower arranging bowl; non-toxic flowers without thorns; foliage; scissors or knife; florist's tape.

Preparation

Place newspaper on the floor and table to protect from pollen or stains. Place the foam to soak in a large bowl of water. Choose flowers, fresh or artificial, with several buds per stem, eg, carnations. Trim the flowers and foliage so that they are ready to be added to an arrangement. Shorter stems will be easier to insert.

Tape the foam in the dish with florist's tape or, for individual arrangements, use yogurt pots. Add a small amount of water to the bowl before decorating begins. When the children have finished, remember to put more water in the bowl.

Activity

Ask who likes flowers. Show some of the flowers and let them smell them. Ask who made the flowers. Remind them that God did. Say you are going to use the flowers and leaves to make (a) beautiful decoration(s).

Help children arrange leaves and then flowers in one large arrangement or in individual pots. Encourage and thank them for all efforts and comment on how beautiful it looks.

If children make a large arrangement, put it on display somewhere, on a welcome desk or the refreshments table, with a sign saying who made it. Top up the flower decorations with water. If they've made their own decorations, remind parents/carers to add water when they get home.

Tell the children that they can take their flowers home to enjoy or give them to someone else to make them happy.

Prayer

Invite the children to point to the different colours as you say them.

Dear God, thank you for all the different flowers: red, yellow, orange, green and white.

Thank you for the lovely colours. Amen.

> ### TOP TIP
>
> Instead of using real flowers, make them from tissue paper with straws for stems. These make ideal Mothering Sunday and Father's Day gifts.

Food collages

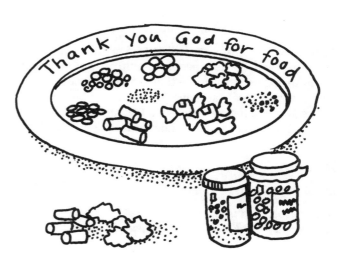

You will need: Thick marker pen; unwaxed paper plates; assortment of dried foods; bowls; spices (in small pots covered with pierced clingfilm); glue and spreaders or glue sticks.

Preparation

Place a selection of dried foods in separate bowls. Set aside some food for a snack afterwards – taking into account any food allergies.

Write on each paper plate, 'Thank you God for food.'

Activity

Get the children to talk about their favourite foods. Show them the dried foods you have brought. What are they? Do they like any of them? Allow them to handle the foods. Next, let them smell the different spices such as cinnamon, garlic, oregano, mint, pepper, etc. Which smells do they like and which don't they like?

Ask if they'd like to make their own food collages. Sprinkle their favourite smells onto the plate and ask the children to rub in the dried spice to give the plate that aroma. Give them time to glue the food onto their plates. Explain that they can't eat what they've glued there, but when everyone is finished, you have a snack to share.

As they work, remind them that God created everything, including food. He uses people to help grow and prepare it for our meals. Encourage them to thank God before they eat their meals at home. To finish, explain that you're going to have a snack in a few minutes, but first you are going to practise a short grace together.

Prayer

Introduce this grace and practise a few times.

God is good. God is great.
Thank you for the food we eat. Amen.

Footprints

You will need: Animal picture-book that shows animals' feet; Post-it notes; shallow bowl; thick water-based poster paint; water; towels; kitchen roll; newspaper; card; foot-washing facilities.

Preparation

In the picture-book, cover the faces of the animals with Post-it notes, so that only their legs and feet are showing. Fill the bowl with paint and place the footwashing facilities and towels close by. Lay newspapers on the floor where the children will be playing.

Activity

Ask the children what their feet look like. Allow them to take off their shoes and socks and show you. Talk about feet and toes – size, width, etc. Say you have a book with pictures of feet in it, but they are not people's feet. Can they guess who the feet belong to? Try to include pictures of snakes or worms that have no feet and caterpillars with lots of feet. As they guess, remove the Post-it note to show the correct answer. As you show them the pictures, point out the shapes and styles of the animals' feet.

Ask if they've ever walked in mud and left a footprint. Point out that we all leave different footprints, depending on the sizes and styles of our shoes. Animals also walk in the mud and leave footprints. Point out that animals' footprints depend on the shape of their feet.

Ask them if they'd like to make a footprint, using paint instead of mud. Those wearing trousers will have to roll them up. Let each child step in the paint and then onto the card. Let them take a few steps round the card, if they want to. They should then step in the bowl to wash their feet, dry them with the towels and put their socks and shoes back on.

Prayer

Invite them to hold up their footprint.

Thank you God for feet and footprints and for the fun we can have running about. Amen.

TOP TIP

While waiting for their turn and waiting for their footprints to dry, children can practise using their feet in any running activity (though not too close to the paint).

Forgetting

You will need: *Basket or box; labels and pen (optional); tray with snacks.*

Preparation

Make sure the floor is clear and safe for children to go without shoes/socks. If the floor is polished, children can slip wearing socks, and bare feet may be safer.

Activity

Talk about shoes and socks. Ask them to take their shoes and/or socks off. Label shoes if you have a large group, and if socks are removed as well, tuck these into shoes. Ask the children to put their shoes in your basket/box.

Ask if they have ever forgotten where they put their shoes. What do they do when they lose their shoes? Where do they look? Have they ever lost anything else? Listen to the answers. Explain that you're going to hide their shoes. Then everyone can help look for the shoes and bring them back to the basket.

Encourage the children to close their eyes as you hide the paired shoes in fairly obvious places. Tell them to open their eyes, find the shoes and bring them back in pairs to the basket/box.

While everyone is putting on shoes and socks again, hide a tray of snacks. Tell them you've forgotten where the snacks are and invite them to find the tray for everyone to share.

Prayer

Thank you God for helping us find things when we forget. Amen.

> ### TOP TIP
> Read *Elmer and the Lost Teddy* by David McKee (Red Fox).

Friendship bracelets

You will need: *Large beads or dried pasta; food colouring; scissors; thin elastic; bodkins.*

Bible links

David and Jonathan: 1 Samuel 20

A friend loves at all times: Proverbs 17:17

Laying down one's life for one's friends: John 15:13

Preparation

If using pasta, you could dye it using food colouring. Cut the elastic into bracelet-length strips and make a sample bracelet by threading pasta/beads onto a piece of elastic.

Activity

Talk about friends and what they do with them: play, talk, go to the park and meet at playgroup. Friends are special. Talk about giving to, and receiving presents from, friends.

Explain that today you're going to make a present for a friend. It's called a friendship bracelet. Show them the sample one. (As the children will probably want to keep their bracelets, they could make two, one for them and one to give to a friend.)

Help the children thread the beads/pasta, then check for size before tying a knot in the elastic to finish. Remind them that when they look at the bracelet, they can remember to thank God for their friends.

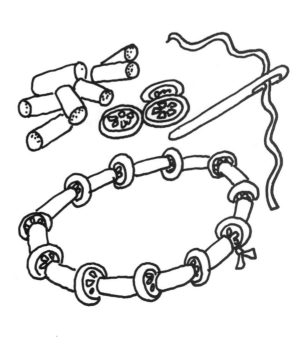

Prayer

Suggest the children touch their bracelets as you pray.

*Dear God, thank you for friends that we can play and
laugh with.*
Help our friends to have a good day. Amen.

Fun with fruit

You will need: *Selection of seasonal fresh fruit (check for
allergies); knife; chopping board; serving bowls; large
bowl; small dishes; handwashing facilities.*

Preparation

Wash and slice the selected fruit, keeping different types
in separate bowls. You may want to leave a whole piece
of fruit of each type with the cut up pieces so that the
children can recognise them easily.

Activity

Explain to the children that you're going to make a
snack together, so first everyone must wash their hands.
Tell them that what you are making today is called fruit
salad. Show them the different fruits, one bowl at a time.
Ask them the names and colours of the fruit and which
ones they like.

Next, invite everyone to sit at the table and give them
each a dish. Explain that they can each take some of the
different fruits and put it in their dishes. When they
have finished adding fruit, they can mix the salad with
their fingers. Talk with them about how it feels in their
fingers and the differences in textures and sizes of the
fruits. Encourage them to pray and eat with you, as
below.

Prayer

Invite the children to eat a piece of fruit as you say
thank you for it. Use the names of the fruits you are
eating.

God, thank you for all kinds of fruit.
Thank you for apples, pears and bananas.
Raisins, plums and oranges are yummy too. Amen.

Fun with play dough

You will need: Play dough; shaping and cutting tools.

Bible Link

Genesis 1: Creation

Activity

Take some time to talk about how amazing we are. Go over the parts of the body with the children including: facial features, legs, arms, stomach, feet, hands and so on. Enjoy a round of 'Head, shoulders, knees and toes'. Note that God made each of us and all the animals and birds too.

Can they think of an animal or a bird or something else that God has made – like a tree or a flower – that they would like to make? Give them some free time with the play dough.

At the end, look together at all the things they have made. Remind them that God made the real thing. Isn't he amazing?

Prayer

Invite the children to give themselves a hug as they say:

Dear God, thank you for making me.

Games

Note: this activity will work best with a small group of children.

You will need: Wide sticky tape (eg, masking tape); dice; age-appropriate board games.

Preparation

You will need quite a bit of space for this activity. Mark out a large grid with gaffer tape. Mark some snakes and ladders between different squares.

Activity

Explain that two children at a time can start at the beginning. Each one rolls the dice in turn and jumps that number of places forward. If they land on a ladder they can follow it to a higher square. If they land on a snake, they must slither down to a lower square. Congratulate them when they reach the end of the game.

While they're waiting for their turn, enjoy playing with the board games.

Prayer

Invite the children to stand on the grid.

Thank you God for games. They're fun! Amen.

Glasses

You will need: *A4 card; scissors; clear plastic paper or acetates; glasses and sunglasses; binoculars; bug boxes; magnifying glasses; books; glue sticks; mirror (optional).*

Bible links

Blind Bartimaeus receives his sight: Mark 10:46–52

Jesus heals a man born blind: John 9:1–41

Preparation

Photocopy the glasses template onto the card and cut out the frame and sides – one for each child – without detaching the sides from the front frame. Using the plastic paper or acetate, cut two circular lenses per pair of glasses.

Activity

Ask the children what we see with. Ask what some people wear to help them see better. If they don't guess, show them a pair of glasses. Ask if they know anyone who wears them. Explain that glasses make things look bigger or clearer. Say that there are other things too that we can use to help us to see, like magnifying glasses, binoculars and bug boxes. Show them these items and how to use them. Allow them time to experiment with the different tools. Remind them to be careful. Allow the children using magnifying glasses to look at the books, for a short time.

Regroup for a Bible story about a man named Bartimaeus. Bartimaeus was blind (that means he couldn't see). One day, Bartimaeus was sitting by the side of the road, when Jesus came along. Bartimaeus shouted out, 'Jesus! Help me!' Jesus stopped and called Bartimaeus. 'What would you like me to do for you, Bartimaeus?' asked Jesus. 'I want to be able to see!' said Bartimaeus. 'Go', said Jesus, 'your eyes are made better because you trusted me.' Suddenly, Bartimaeus could see. He could see the sun and the trees and the people. And most importantly he could see Jesus.

Next, explain that you're going to make pretend glasses. Help children decorate their frames and glue on the plastic paper. Let them try on their glasses and if possible, provide mirrors so that they can see themselves. Explain that when they look at their glasses, they can remember that God gave us eyes to see things with and that Jesus made Bartimaeus' eyes better.

Prayer

Invite the children to put on their glasses as they pray and copy your actions.

Dear God, thank you for our eyes
  (place their hands over their glasses)
and that we can see
  (uncover their glasses).
Please help people, like Bartimaeus, who can't. Amen.

TOP TIP

Play 'Pin the tail on the donkey'. Remember that many young children don't like wearing blindfolds so don't force them. Instead suggest that they close their eyes very tightly before pinning the tail on the donkey.

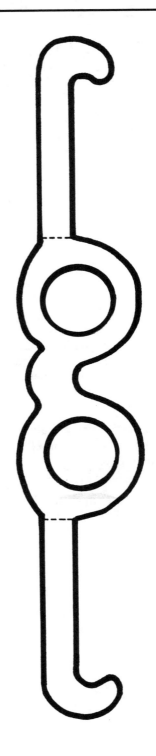

Go, go, go!

You will need: Selection of different transport toys; dolls; buggies; plastic or carpet street layout for toy vehicles.

Activity

Show the children all the toys. Ask them what you do with them. Encourage them to say they help us go to places. Let children tell you where they like to go and how they get there. Point to the appropriate transport. Invite them to make sounds or sing songs about each object, eg, *'choo choo'* for the train, *'brrm brrm'* for the car, *'zoom'* for the plane and 'The wheels on the bus' for the bus.

Allow some free time to play with the different toys, then gather the children and ask them each to bring over one of the toys they were playing with. If there are not enough to go round, ask them to help each other by carrying the toys together. Ask the children what type of toy they each have. Encourage the older ones to answer for the younger ones who cannot. For the child with the doll, explain that their way of getting about is their feet and that we all use our feet to help us to get to places every day, even if it is just to the kitchen or the bathroom.

Prayer

As you pray, invite each child to hold one toy. When you mention that toy, they can drive it into the centre of the circle. Mention the toys in pairs, eg, lorries and bicycles.

Dear God, we thank you for cars and bikes. We thank you for all the places aeroplanes and buses can take us. We pray that you'll be with all the people who ride in buggies and on tractors and that you'll keep them safe. Amen.

God keeps his promises

You will need: Baby dolls: blankets; basket; male doll dressed as adult; female doll dressed as adult; towel.

Bible link

God's covenant with Abram: Genesis 15:5–6

The birth of Isaac: Genesis 21:1–7

Preparation

Wrap one baby doll in the blanket and place it in the basket. Cover it with a towel or sheet, so the children cannot see it. Place the extra babies and blankets out of the way.

Activity

Introduce the children to Abram (boy doll) and his wife Sarah (girl doll). They loved God very much and God loved them. Ask the children to help you imitate the dolls saying, 'We love you God.'

God promised Abram and Sarah that they would have a baby. They were very excited. Encourage the children to show excitement. So, they waited, but there was no baby. And they waited some more. And Abram and Sarah waited some more. They did a lot of waiting but they had no baby. It was time for them to move house. *(Invite the children to walk with you to the new house.)*

Now Sarah and Abram were getting old, so they had to walk more slowly. *(Walk more and more slowly with the children and then slowly sit down.)* And they waited some more. They wondered why God had promised them a baby and they hadn't got one.

But one day, to everyone's surprise, Sarah had a baby! *(Show them the baby doll and explain they named him Isaac.)* Ask them how they think Abram and Sarah felt. Say they were very happy. God had said they would have a baby and God kept his promise! *(Invite the children to play with the other baby dolls and give them names.)*

Prayer

Dear God, we thank you that you keep your promises. Sarah and Abram had their baby Isaac. Help us to wait; we know you keep your promises. Amen.

God loves me

You will need: Cheap wigs (from a fancy dress shop); hats; glasses; trainers; boots; shoes; mirrors; Polaroid camera (optional).

Bible link

The hairs of your head are numbered: Luke 12:7

Preparation

Place some mirrors about the room in safe yet accessible places. Assemble dressing-up clothes.

Activity

Talk about hair and eye-colour and height. Explain that God made us all to look different, with brown, black and blonde hair and blue, green and brown eyes. Sometimes we can pretend to change our hair colour with wigs and hats. We can look different by wearing different sorts of shoes, eg, sandals or wellies. Allow time for free play with the dressing-up items. Encourage the children to look at themselves in the mirrors. If you have a Polaroid camera you could take a few pictures. After taking off the dressing up-clothes, the children can look in the mirror and compare themselves to the picture.

Gather the children together again and ask them to shake their heads when you call out their hair colour – red, brown, blonde and black. Remind them that God made us all look different. None of us look exactly alike, but God loves us just the same.

Prayer

Invite the children to say the rhyme and do the actions with you.

God loves my hair (Touch hair.)
when it's short (Hands close to head.)
and when it's long. (Hands far from head.)
God loves me with glasses (Make circles around the eyes.)
and without. (Take their hands away.)
God loves me when I'm small, (Crouch down.)
God loves me when I'm tall, (Stand on tiptoes.)
God loves me just the way I am! (Jump up.) *Amen.*

God's special box

You will need: Boxes (shoebox size, one for each child); pictures of cherubim (two per child); plastic jewels; gold glitter or glitter glue; glue sticks; shiny paper; stickers; felt-tip pens or crayons.

Bible link

The Ark (God's special box): Exodus 25:10–22

Activity

Explain to the children that long ago in the Bible, when a man named Moses was alive, they didn't have lots of churches, like we have today. They only had one. In this church was God's special box. God told Moses how to build the box and decorate it, so that it would be kept special. They were to add gold, four rings, and two angels on the outside to decorate it. Inside the box, they kept things that reminded them of what God had done for them.

Show them your boxes and invite them to decorate one each like God's special box. Help them decorate the boxes with angels, jewels, glitter and shiny paper. Explain that they can keep special things in the boxes and remember the good things that God has done.

Prayer

Invite the children to hold up their boxes.

Thank you God for special things.
Help us to take care of the special things you give us.
Amen.

Good Food

You will need: Chocolate brownie cake-mix, or recipe and ingredients; baking trays/tins; fat for greasing; kitchen roll; handwashing facilities; raisins and other edible decorations; paper plates or napkins; drink; cups; small bowls and plastic kitchen utensils; mixing bowls; aprons; oven; wire cooling racks.

Preparation

Use a cake-mix or a brownie recipe that you trust (check for allergies and avoid baking with nuts). Decide how you are going to divide up your group for this session, and weigh out and measure ingredients accordingly. Set everything out beforehand in a way that is easy for children to use. Switch on the oven. Make sure the children are kept well away from the oven.

Activity

When the children arrive, ask if they'd like to do some cooking today. Explain that first everyone must wash their hands and put on aprons. Let them help grease the trays and then mix the ingredients. Finally, add additional decorations such as raisins, chocolate chips or other nut-free sweets. Put the brownies in the oven to bake.

While the cake is baking, ask the children to help you set the table with plates/napkins and cups.

Allow them some free play in a play kitchen or with safe kitchen items, while the brownies finish baking. Cool on wire racks before letting children taste what they have cooked.

Prayer

Dear God, we thank you for good food to eat.
Help us always to share, like we are now. Amen.

Growing seeds

You will need: Newspaper; child's watering can; water; flower or vegetable seeds and pictures from the seed packets; compost; small plant pots or polystyrene cups; thick marker pen.

Bible Link

The parable of the sower: Matthew 13:1–43; Luke 8:1–5

Preparation

Place the newspaper on the floor to catch spilt compost. Fill the watering can with water. Plant and water your own seed. Decide what to do about watering the planted seeds between group meetings.

Activity

Ask who likes being in the garden or playing in the grass. See if they've ever planted any seeds in their gardens. Show them pictures on the seed packets. Explain that you're going to plant some seeds and hopefully they will grow into plants like the ones on the packets. Show the children your planted seed as an example.

Label each plant pot or polystyrene cup with each child's name. Plant the seeds with the children, following the directions on the packet. Water the pots. Plant a few 'spares' in case some don't germinate.

Come back to the plants each week to see how they're growing. Thank God each time for all the growth.

Prayer

Invite the children to start in a squatting position. As the prayer goes on, they can slowly grow and then burst upwards.

God, thank you for g-r-o-w-i-n-g (Say slowly as the children grow.) *seeds.* (Burst upwards by jumping and extending their arms over their heads.) *Amen.*

> ### TOP TIP
> You could link this prayer with a Harvest service, either planting items on this day or growing something for it. Alternatively, you could link it to Jesus' parable of the sower (Matthew 13:1–9 and Luke 8:4–8).

Having fun together

You will need: No items needed.

Activity

Talk to the children about what games they like playing. Games are a great way to have fun with our friends. In a large group circle, play a couple of active games such as 'The farmer's in his den', 'Hokey-cokey' or a version of 'Big floppy teddy bears'. This is a wonderful game which needs no equipment and causes great hilarity! Get everyone to act out being whatever amazing things you can think of, so that you all move around like big floppy teddy bears or smart wooden soldiers or great big elephants or whatever it is that you've chosen. March/flop/dance along to any merry tune and the (variable) words. For example:

Great big elephants dancing along, dancing along, dancing along,

Great big elephants dancing along, dancing along the road (or 'around the room' or whatever your venue).

Prayer

Invite the children to hold hands and skip in a circle as they sing to the tune of 'Ring o'roses'.

Thank you for our friends and
the fun we have together.
Playing, playing,
We all can share.

Hearts

You will need: Biscuit dough (check for allergies); red tissue paper; red card; scissors; heart-shaped cutters; small rolling pins; baking trays; sprinkles or sugar; serving plate; paper ribbon; marker pens; felt-tip pens or crayons; hole punch; aprons; handwashing facilities; oven; cooling racks.

Bible link

The greatest commandment: Matthew 22:34–40; John 13:34

God so loved the world: John 3:16–21

Preparation

Make the biscuit dough. From the tissue paper, cut large hearts to wrap the biscuits in – one per child (use the largest heart-shaped cutter as a rough guide to size). Cut heart-shaped labels from red card and punch a hole in each. Set out the dough and rolling pins, turn on the oven. Make sure the children are kept well away from the oven.

Activity

Show the children one of the cut-out hearts. Ask them what it means. Explain that sometimes we use a heart to say, 'I love you.' Ask the children who they love. Answers may range from Mummy and Daddy to their hamster. Ask the children to tell you the people who love them. Listen to their answers and say that God also loves each of them very much.

Explain that God wants us to love him *(Point upwards.)* and to love other people. *(Point around the room.)* We can do that by being kind to others, even if they're not kind to us. See if the children can suggest ways of showing love. Ask if they'd like to help make heart-shaped biscuits to share with other people.

Make sure they wash hands and put on aprons before rolling and cutting the dough. Make enough dough for them to sample the biscuits themselves as well as taking some home. Help them decorate their biscuits with sprinkles or sugar and bake.

While the biscuits are baking, invite the children to decorate their little heart labels. Remind them that some people like to draw little red hearts to show love. When biscuits are cool enough, let the children help you put two or three biscuits in the red tissue paper. Wrap it around the biscuit and tie the label to the parcel with the paper ribbon. Place the remaining biscuits on a plate and share.

Prayer

Invite the children to sit in a heart shape, instead of a circle.

Sing '*Jesus loves me this I know*'

TOP TIP

Read *Guess How Much I Love You* by Sam McBratney, illustrated by Anita Jeram (Candlewick Books).

I can help

You will need: *Toys; books; play kitchen items; dressing-up clothes; bookshelf or book box; toy box or basket; small brooms and dustpans; toy vacuum cleaners; dusters.*

Preparation

Scatter some toys around the room: take the books off the bookshelf, place the toys outside the basket, put the play kitchen items all round the room, and unfold the clothes. Set up an area as a pretend cupboard with brooms, dustpans, toy vacuum cleaners and dusters.

Activity

Walk around the room with the children and ask them what they see. Agree with them that the room isn't very tidy or clean: toys, clothes and books everywhere and not in their proper places.

Ask if they'd be your helpers and tidy up when they've finished playing. Allow them time to play, then gather them together again and ask them to be your helpers now. If the group is big, divide them into teams. Encourage them to help sort out and tidy up. Lastly, ask if they could help you sweep the floor. Let each child use the brooms, toy vacuum cleaners and dustpans. If you don't have such toys, give them all dusters. Thank them for their help.

Prayer

While still holding the brooms, invite them to have one more sweep around saying:

Thank you God that I can help. Amen.

Leaves

(an autumn activity)

You will need: *Leaves; outdoor area if possible; assistants; A4 card and glue sticks (optional).*

Preparation

Choose a safe, clean, nearby outdoor area with leaves. If there are not many leaves, gather a bag of leaves elsewhere and scatter around your chosen site. If there are no ideal sites, scatter the leaves inside.

Activity

Tell the children to get ready to go out to look for leaves. Before leaving the building, remind them to remain with their parent, carer or assigned assistant. Walk to the area you have selected. You could sing or play 'Follow my leader' en route. When you arrive, remind the children again that they must stay with their parent, carer or assistant.

Show the children a leaf. What is it? Where did it come from? Explain that after the summer lots of leaves fall off trees. Encourage them to collect some leaves to take back with them. On your return, ask the children what they found. Let them hold up their big and small leaves and tell you the colours. The children can take their leaves home as they are, or glue them onto card. Make sure the children wash their hands after handling the leaves.

Prayer

Invite them to wave their leaves as they say:

Thank you God for leaves. Amen.

TOP TIP
You could also make one big outline of a tree on a large piece of card and let children stick their leaves onto the branches to make a poster.

Lego homes

You will need: Lego, Duplo or large building blocks; pictures of houses and interiors.

Preparation

If you haven't got blocks, use cardboard boxes from the supermarket and tape the sides shut.

Activity

Encourage the children to talk about their homes: the colour of their room, if they share it with a brother or sister, where they keep their toys, etc. Show the children some pictures of houses – an architecture or interior decorating magazine or book should have examples. Encourage them to comment on the pictures. Suggest the children build their own homes and allow them some free time with the blocks.

Spend some time looking and talking with them about their buildings. Who might live there? What's inside and what would they do in the house? To finish, ask everyone to help build one big home for everyone to go inside. If using Lego or Duplo, a small perimeter wall will suffice.

Invite all the children into the big house for a prayer.

Prayer

Invite each child to touch a block, as you pray.

Dear God, thank you very much for my home, where I can eat, sleep and play. Amen.

TOP TIP
Discuss other types of homes such as nests, caves and the sea.

Let your light shine

You will need: Table lamps; card or cardboard tubes; sticky tape or glue; shiny paper or tinfoil; torches; a lantern; felt-tip pens or crayons; scissors.

Bible link

Jesus if the light: John 1:4–5

The lamp of the body: Luke 11:33–36

Preparation

Place the lamps around the room, plug in and switch on. To make toy torches, roll pieces of card into a tube and glue or tape together. Alternatively, use cardboard tubes. Cut small circles of shiny paper or tinfoil to be the torch ends and stick or draw on pretend buttons.

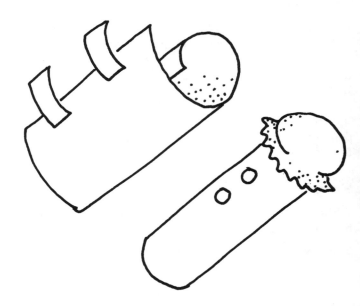

Activity

Ask the children what makes the room so bright. Point out the lamps, lights and even the lantern.

Invite them to see what happens when you turn some lights off. Turn off a few. Ask what happens to the room. See what the children think and how they feel. Ask them to think of times when it is dark. If it's dark can we see anything?

Switch on the torch and point it upwards. Turn the rest of the lamps and lights off, except for one: for safety reasons, you should always have at least a dim light on. Ask the children what the room looks like now. Agree that it's more difficult to see things, but that our eyes do slowly get used to the dark.

Remind them that God is always with us, whether the lights are on or not.

Let children play with the torches. Allow them time to explore the room with their torch (but don't allow them to shine real torches in each other's faces).

If desired, the children can decorate the card rolls or cardboard tubes and use them as pretend torches.

Prayer

Invite the children to turn their torches on and off whenever you say 'light' and 'dark'.

Practise a few times before the prayer.

Thank you God for dark and thank you for light.
Please be with us when it's light and when it's dark.
Help us not be scared of the dark or the light. Amen.

TOP TIP

Read *Can't you Sleep, Little Bear?* by Martin Waddell, illustrated by Barbara Firth (Walker Books).

Long-jump praying

You will need: Themed pictures; masking tape; A4 paper; felt-tip pens or crayons.

Preparation

Using teaching magazines, trace various pictures that can be coloured in. Suggestions include: church, family, playgrounds, houses, animals and plants. Alternatively, let children draw their own pictures. Put down a piece of masking tape as the jumping line.

Activity

Ask the children to help colour some special pictures to be used in a little while. Allow them to choose a picture. (You can use this activity with different themes by varying the pictures you use.) Alternatively, allow the children to draw pictures. As they draw, you could ask what they are drawing and label the picture. When the pictures are finished, divide the children into small groups of three to five. Line each group's pictures up on the floor like a ruler, at right angles to the jumping line.

Encourage each group to stand in a queue behind the jumping line, in such a way that when they jump they land *beside* the pictures. Let children jump in turn. When they land, they say thank you to God for whatever is on the picture they are closest to, then go to the back of the queue. Once everyone has jumped, mix up the line of pictures, as some of the children may land in the same place each time.

Prayer

Invite the children to practise jumping. Then, teach them to say, 'Thank you God.' Lastly, encourage them to say, 'Thank you God,' as they jump.

Thank you God! (Jump.)
Amen. (Final jump.)

Making people welcome

You will need: Dolls; teddy bears.

Activity

Introduce yourself to the children. Ask if they know who you are and who everyone else is. Invite them to take turns saying their names. Encourage everyone else to say 'Hello (name)' and wave. Ask the children how else we can say hello to new people. Offer them suggestions to agree or disagree with such as: smiling, saying, 'Hello', sharing your toys, pouting, taking toys away, yelling at people.

Invite them to practise the positive ways – say 'hello', smile, share a toy, wave, shake hands, hug, and any other ideas they have. Encourage them to get up and walk around, meeting everyone in a friendly way. After this, explain that we forgot to introduce some people. Point to the dolls and teddy bears. Ask if they'd like to introduce the dolls or teddy bears to the group. Allow them time to practise the welcoming gestures they've learned.

Prayer

Invite the children to join you in the actions and words of the short rhyme.

Thank you God for new friends. We can shake hello (Shake hands.) *and wave goodbye.* (Wave.) *Amen.*

Megaphone prayers

You will need: *Megaphone; A4 card; sticky tape; small beanbags; felt-tip pens or crayons.*

Preparation

Make a sample megaphone or borrow a real one. To make a megaphone, roll the A4 card into a large cone shape and tape the sides.

Activity

Show the children the megaphone. Encourage discussion about what it is and what it's for.

Talk through it as a clue and let them have a turn too. Ask if they would like to make their own megaphones. Let them decorate the card for the megaphones. Then roll and tape together.

Ask who might use a megaphone and why. Let them practise their suggested scenarios. Another option is a mini sports day. Let them try several activities and use their megaphones to announce how well they did, eg, they could practise the long jump and then call out where they landed. Next, have a short race. When they reach the finishing line, encourage them to call out their names. Then, have a beanbag throw. Once everyone has had a chance to throw, let them run down and collect their beanbag, stating how far it went. (Don't let children run while someone is throwing in the same direction.) Lastly, let them lie on their stomachs and pretend to swim. They can let everyone know when they reach the end of the pool. Conclude the sports day by using your megaphone to congratulate everyone. Remind them that megaphones are loud and help us get people's attention.

Prayer

Invite the children to repeat after you through their megaphones:

Thank you God that we can be noisy and have fun. Amen.

Mixed feelings

You will need: Wool; scissors; a selection of picture story books about how people feel; small, unwaxed paper plates – two for each child; small circles of felt – at least six per child; short smooth sticks; glue sticks or glue; felt-tip pens or crayons.

Bible link

Oh Lord … you know me: Psalm 139

Preparation

Cut the wool into assorted lengths for hair for the paper plate puppets. Select some books to look at. Choose ones where the characters express several emotions, eg, *I Want My Potty* by Tony Ross (Picture Lions) and *Bartholomew Bear* by Virginia Miller (Walker Books).

Activity

Invite the children to join you in looking at the pictures in the books. Ask the children what the people in the pictures are doing and how they are feeling. Then let children explain why they think the character feels like that. Encourage them to talk about times when they have felt happy/sad/angry. Explain that God loves each one of us. He made us and knows what we think and how we feel. When we pray to God, we can tell him how we feel.

Help the children to make paper plate puppets. Explain they can make two to show the different ways they sometimes feel. They can use the wool for hair, felt circles for eyes and noses and draw mouths. Lastly glue the short smooth sticks to the puppets as handles.

Encourage them all to hold up one, then the other puppet. Finally, read one of the stories. Encourage the children to hold up the appropriate puppet depending on the character's feelings. Give them time to play with their puppets.

Prayer

As you pray, invite them to hold up the appropriate puppet.

Dear God, thank you for making all of us, even our feelings. When we're sad, please be with us. When we're happy, thank you that we can smile and always tell you how we feel. Amen.

> ## TOP TIP
> You can also use socks for puppets.

Mobile families

You will need: Clip art pictures or pictures of family members; hole punch; paper ribbon; felt-tip pens or crayons; card; plastic coat hangers; sticky tape; picture of your family.

Preparation

Photocopy clip art pictures of family members: baby, sister, brother, mother, father, grandmother, grandfather, aunt, uncle, cat, dog, hamster and fish onto thin card. Alternatively, you could let the children draw their own family members. Punch holes in the top of each picture. Cut five or six strands of ribbon per child. If you need to use wire coat hangers, cover the sharp ends with tape. Make a sample mobile of your family.

Activity

Show the children your family photograph. Tell them a little bit about your family and let the children tell you about theirs. Show your mobile and explain that it helps you remember to pray for your family. Ask if they'd like to make mobiles too. Get the children to select pictures representing their different family members. Don't worry if they want a picture of a pet or a relative you know they don't have. If necessary, let the children colour them in.

When the children have finished colouring in their pictures, help them thread the paper ribbon through the holes and tie to the hanger. As you tie each bow, invite the child to hold the mobile with you and say: 'Thank you God for my family.' If they are too shy, say the child's name instead of 'my'. Encourage them to take their family mobiles home and remember to pray for their families.

Prayer

When everyone's mobile is complete, encourage the children to hold them up in the air as a sign of lifting them up to God.

Dear God, we thank you for our families and how much they love us. Amen.

> ## TOP TIP
> Mobiles can also be made with pictures of pets and food, seashells, buttons, stars, bells or other ideas you have to suit the theme or event.

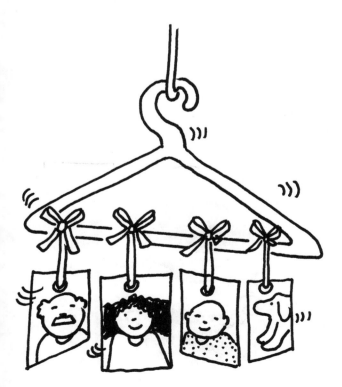

Model churches

You will need: *Newspapers; play dough; play dough shaping and cutting tools; short smooth sticks; pictures of different buildings associated with churches: school buildings; house; church hall; grassy area/churchyard.*

Preparation

Spread newspaper to protect the area where the children will use the play dough.

Activity

If you meet in a church, ask the children if they know what the building is called. Explain it's called a church. If you don't meet in a church, show the children a picture of a more traditional church. Then, show the children different pictures of other churches. Explain that people meet to worship God in different sorts of churches. Some meet in school buildings or people's homes. In hot countries, they meet outside.

If you meet in a church, take the children on a tour of the building, drawing attention to special parts of your church and what happens there. (If you don't meet in a church, why not arrange a trip to a local church with the group?) While touring the church, explain that church buildings are important but not as important to God as the people who come to them to worship him.

When you return from the tour, talk with the children about what they liked best. Allow them time to make their own churches using play dough. They could use the short smooth sticks as steeples. Remind them that God likes churches, but he loves people even more.

Prayer

Here's the church,
   (Interlock fingers.)
Here's the steeple,
   (Point index fingers upwards.)
Open the doors,
   (Open thumbs.)
And here's the people!
   (Flip hands upside down and wiggle fingers.)
Thank you God that we can go to church and learn about you. Amen.

> **TOP TIP**
> Pray for the people who help in churches and the people who attend (John 17:6–19 and Ephesians 6:18).

Mountains and hills

You will need: *Picture storybooks with mountains and hills.*

Bible link

At Mount Sinai: Exodus 19

Preparation

Choose some storybooks with pictures of mountains and hills.

Activity

Show the children some pictures of mountains and hills. Ask if any of them have ever climbed a big hill. Sing 'Jack and Jill went up the hill' while pretending to climb. Then march round singing 'The Grand Old Duke of York' improvising some actions, eg, stretching arms high for 'when they were up' and crouching down as they march for 'when they were down'.

Ask if any of them have seen a mountain. Allow them to share any experiences and tales. Show some more pictures and point out the types of animals that like to live there. Explain there was once was a man named Moses who had to walk all the way up a mountain to talk to God. Remind them that we don't have to climb mountains or go somewhere special to talk to God. We can do that anywhere.

Prayer

Thank you God that we can pray to you anywhere,
Up a mountain,
   (Walk their fingers up.)
Or at the bottom of the mountain.
   (Walk their fingers down.)
Amen.

Moving about

You will need: Mats or carpet (if floors are hard).

Important note

If you have someone in your group with a disability, use this activity with great sensitivity: warn the parent/carer well in advance, asking their advice, and if possible allow the child with a disability to demonstrate any special skills, such as manoeuvring a wheelchair.

Preparation

Put down mats/carpet if needed.

Activity

Ask the children to show you how many things they can do with their legs and feet – hopping, jogging or running. Next see what they can do with their arms. Try stretching up, twisting from side-to-side and touching their toes. Ask the children if babies can do all those things. Invite them to lie on their backs and pretend to be babies. Let them put their feet in the air, slowly wiggle their little toes, their big toes, their legs, then their whole bodies. Finally see who can put their legs back on the floor and stay completely still for ten seconds.

Explain that some people stay completely still because they *can't* move. Just as little babies need a lot of help, some adults do too. Remind the children that those of us who can move about can help those who can't, like little babies, younger brothers and sisters, and others.

Prayer

Invite the children to lie on the mats and wriggle for the first line and then stay still for the second line.

Dear God, thank you for our arms and legs and all the things we can do with them.
Help us always to be ready to help other people who can't do as much as we can. Amen.

TOP TIP

Sing 'Hokey-cokey' or 'Father Abraham'.

Moving house

You will need: Boxes (large enough to sit in – two per child); felt-tip pens or crayons.

Bible link

Ruth and Naomi: Ruth 1–4

Preparation

Cut away the top flaps of the boxes. The children should be able to sit in them or hide under them while pretending the box is their house. (You can sometimes get boxes big enough to cut doors and windows in from warehouses or shops.) Set up two separate areas of 'houses' in different parts of the room.

Activity

As the children arrive, invite them to inspect the pretend houses. Ask if they look like their own homes. Allow them a few minutes to share with you the differences between the two. Invite them to sit in the houses in one area while listening to a story from the Bible.

There was once a woman named Ruth who lived with a very nice woman called Naomi in a place called Moab. There was not enough food for everyone so Naomi decided to move to a new place called Bethlehem, where there was more food.

Invite the children to travel to Bethlehem, like Ruth and Naomi, by moving to the boxes in the second area of the room. Encourage them to settle in their new homes. Ask what they might do when they move into a new house. Pretend to do the things the children suggest, like unpacking and meeting the neighbours. Explain that in Bethlehem, Ruth didn't know anyone. Ruth had never lived in Bethlehem before. Ask the children how Ruth may have felt.

She was probably scared and felt… *(Ask the children for suggestions.)* But God was with Ruth. She worked on a farm and made a very special friend. His name was Boaz and they got married. Remind them that God was with Ruth and he will always be with us, no matter where we live.

Allow the children to decorate the boxes to take home.

Prayer

Invite the children to sit in their houses as you pray.

Dear God, thank you that you are always with us.
No matter where we go or live. Amen.

TOP TIP

If you cannot obtain boxes, make 'dens' using chairs back to back with a blanket or sheet draped over them.

Musical praise

You will need: *Boxes; seeds; paper plates or cups; pasta; cardboard tubes; bells; scissors; songbooks; felt-tip pens or crayons; glue sticks or sticky tape; musical instruments suitable for children such as a child's keyboard, guitar, triangle, shakers, drums and bells.*

Bible links

I will yet praise him: Psalm 43:5

I will praise you: Psalm 63:4

Praise the Lord: Romans 15:11

The sacrifice of praise: Hebrews 13:15

Activity

Ask the children if they like making music, ask how they can do it. Show them some child-friendly musical instruments, such as those listed above. Show them the songbooks, explaining that they help people know what sounds to play and what words to sing.

Encourage the children to try out the instruments. Remind them that they can also make sounds with their bodies by tapping their feet, clapping their hands and clicking their fingers. Practise doing these things.

Say they can make their own musical instruments to take home, by placing seeds in a packet between two paper plates or cups taped together, or by adding dried pasta to a box and taping it closed. They could also add bells to a cardboard tube, place raisins in a plastic bottle, and make card megaphones.

Let them make some instruments. Get adults to help the children select different items to add to containers. Allow the children some free time playing their instruments and looking at the songbooks. Then get them to play their instruments while you sing some songs together such as 'God is so good'.

Prayer

Suggest that the children make some music as their prayer to God.

Dear God, thank you that we can make music.
   (Pause for them to make music.)
Amen. (Shout.)

> ### TOP TIP
>
> *Let's Sing and Shout!* and *Let's all clap hands!* both edited by Maggie Barfield (SU) contains praise songs and rhymes. For Christian praise music, try *Great Big God* (Vineyard Music, UK).

Safety note

Make sure that boxes, plates, etc, are securely sealed so that the small items inside can't escape.

Noah's Ark

You will need: Towels; large bowls or baby bath; water; kitchen roll/extra towels; plastic boats; funnels; jugs; aprons; Noah's ark story such as Come into the Ark with Noah *by Stephanie Jeffs and Chris Saunderson (SU).*

Bible link

The Flood: Genesis 6–9

Preparation

Lay towels or newspaper on the floor where you will do the activity. Put water in the bowls/baby bath and place on tables or towels/newspapers. Place extra hand towels or kitchen roll within easy reach, but far enough away not to get splashed.

Activity

Ask if they have ever seen a boat or been on one. Allow them to tell you about their experiences.

Say that a man called Noah built an ark which was like a big boat. Show the children the plastic boats and let them handle them. Tell them that when Noah was in his boat it rained for 40 days without stopping! (If you have four children in the group, let them each hold up their fingers to show how many 40 is.) So Noah had to spend 40 days living on a boat.

Let the children wear aprons to put the boats in the water and play. Point out that water moves in waves. Encourage them to make small waves too. Let them use funnels and jugs to rain on the boats. Ask the children to dry their hands and move somewhere else to listen to the story. As they do so, move the bowl and boats out of the way.

Prayer

Each child can hold a boat.

Dear God, thank you for boats and for keeping Noah safe in his special ark. Amen.

Safety note

Remember that young children can drown in just a few centimetres of water. NEVER leave children unattended near water.

TOP TIP
You could bring in a small inflatable boat for the children to sit in on dry ground.

Paper chains

You will need: *Sheets of A4 coloured paper; scissors; sticky tape; glue sticks; glitter; felt-tip pens or crayons; party blowers; party snack.*

Preparation

Take a sheet of A4 paper and cut widthways to make eight equal strips (each strip will be approximately 21 x 3.5 cm). You need one sheet of coloured paper cut into strips for each child. Decorate and interlink a few strips as a sample.

Activity

Ask the children if they have ever been to a party. Let them tell you about it. Ask if they'd like to have a party and help you make some decorations. Show the children the paper chains you've made and say they can make some more.

Let the children decorate their links with glitter and felt-tip pens before gluing them. They could each make a short chain or the whole group could make a longer one together. If they make individual chains, label them so that they take their own home. Finally, get the children to help you set out some party items, such as blowers, balloons and food. Enjoy the party!

Prayer

If the children have made short chains, invite them to spin or twirl them as you pray.

Thank you God for parties and the fun we had. Amen.

Paper people

You will need: *A4 paper (white or coloured), cut in half lengthways; felt-tip pens; scissors.*

Preparation

Fold the strips concertina-fashion so that you have four folded edges: the folds need to be accurate so it may be easiest to fold the strip in half, then in half twice more, before refolding it concertina-style using the fold-lines as a guide. Draw a simple outline of a person on the top side, with hands and feet touching the fold (this is essential). Cut round the outline carefully, leaving hands and feet intact at the fold. Unfold for 'zigzag' people. In advance, prepare as many of these as you have children in the group, but leave a couple to cut out in front of the children as they like to see the people appear as you unfold the paper.

Activity

Give each child one set of paper people. Label with their names. Remind them to unfold them gently. Let the children decorate their people using felt-tip pens.

Prayer

Dear God, thank you for the fun we can have with paper people. Amen.

TOP TIP

You can also make concertina snowmen or fir trees for a seasonal activity.

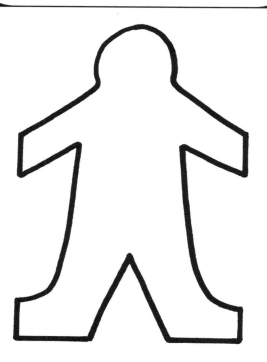

Pass the parcel

You will need: *Bags of sweets; wrapping paper; sticky tape; music and CD/cassette player; twists of tissue paper or small paper bags.*

Preparation

Select enough sweets for each child in the group to have one per round, and then wrap the rest in a paper bag or a twist of tissue in the first layer of wrapping paper. If you prefer you could use small stickers instead of sweets. Place as many sweets as you have children in each layer of paper, ensuring there are enough layers for each child to have a go. If you have a large group, you could have two circles of children and two parcels. Place the CD/cassette player near you.

Activity

Turn the music on and invite the children to sit in a circle. Ask them if they've ever received a parcel or present in the post. What did they get? Explain that you're going to play pass the parcel. When the music is playing they should pass the parcel from one to another. When the music stops, the child holding the parcel can unwrap one layer and share what's inside with everybody. Stress that the present in each layer is for sharing with the whole group.

Prayer

Invite them to scrunch up a piece of the wrapping paper as you say:

God, thank you for presents and that we can all share!

Pavement prayers

You will need: *A safe paved area, preferably enclosed or dark construction paper; coloured chalks; water; bucket and detergent.*

Preparation

Obtain permission to chalk on the pavement and find out whether or not the children's art can be left. If you can't find a suitable paved area outside, you can do this indoors using dark construction paper: tape sheets to the floor to look like a narrow pavement. Using white chalk, draw paving stones on the construction paper.

Activity

Show the children the pavement or ask them what the construction paper looks like. Have they ever tried hopping over the cracks in a pavement? Allow them some time to show you, or try a round of hopscotch. Ask if they'd like to help you decorate these few pavement stones. Explain that they can't usually decorate paving stones, but you asked for permission to decorate these. Allow the children to chalk on the pavement. At the end let them admire their efforts by walking or hopping around, still not stepping on the cracks. If you do this activity in church, you could wait until people have seen the children's artwork before you wash it off.

Prayer

Invite the children to start at one end of the pavement and hop or jump along, next to their artwork.

For each hop/jump, they can say, *'Thank you for…'*
On their last hop/jump, they can say, *'Amen.'*

Pet blessings

You will need: *Photographs of the children's pets; small live pets in cages; book about pet animals.*

Preparation

The week before, encourage the children to bring in a photograph of their pet(s) or a pet in a cage. Check with parents/carers so that you know what to expect. Also check for allergies and ensure that no child with an allergy comes into contact with the pets.

Activity

Gather the children away from the area with the caged pets. Ask the children who has pets. Allow them to show you the photographs. You can also look through a picture book so that children who forgot their photos, or those who do not have a pet, can point to the one they have or would like to have.

Encourage the children to practise animal noises as you look at the photos and book. Next ask those who have brought their pets if they would like to show them to the group. Say that you'll place the pets around the room with an assistant or carer, so they can walk around to see each other's pets. Ensure that children are very careful with the pets, and keep children away from any pet that might bite. Remind them God created everything, including our pets, and that God knows how happy our pets make us and wants us to take care of them.

Prayer

Dear God, we thank you for pets,
Big and little, furry and scaly. Amen.

> **TOP TIP**
> Arrange a trip to the zoo, a children's farm or pet shop.

Picnic walk

You will need: *Picnic basket; little sandwiches (check for allergies); napkins; cups; children's flasks or water bottles; squash or water; picnic rug.*

Preparation

Pack the picnic basket with the sandwiches, napkins and cups. Fill the flasks or small water bottles with water or drink.

Activity

Explain to the children that you'd like to go on a picnic. Invite them to join you. To get there, explain that you'll have to go on a pretend journey through the forest. Ask them to check that their shoes are on tight. Pretend to put on coats and hats in case it's cold. Invite them to take a deep breath because it's a long way. Ask them to help you carry some picnic supplies, like their own flasks and the rug.

Begin the journey by walking in zigzags. Sing some marching songs. Warn the children about 'obstacles'. They might need to walk over a bridge, step over branches, move rocks out of the way and slide around trees. Ask if anyone is tired yet. They may want to take a break on their pretend journey and have a drink.

Get ready for the rest of the journey. It could involve some climbing, leaping and hopping on rocks over a stream. Finally, everyone gets to the big grassy space for the picnic. Spread out the rug, say a short thank you prayer to God and enjoy the picnic. Reverse the order to get back home.

Prayer

Thank you for our picnic and helping us get here. Amen.

> **TOP TIP**
> Enjoy an outdoor picnic at a safe, local park.

Picture frames

You will need: *Thick A5 card (or cardboard picture holders); craft knife; ruler; glue stick; framed photographs of your family; flower petals; pasta; large buttons; milk bottle tops; stickers; glitter; felt-tip pens or crayons; string or magnets (optional).*

Preparation

If you are not using cardboard picture holders, use a craft knife and a ruler to cut a large rectangle out of the centre of a piece of A5-sized card, leaving a 3 cm border all round. Put glue around three of the four edges and glue a second piece of card to the back. Leave one side unglued to slide the photograph in. (A frame like this using A5 card takes a standard photo – approximately 15 x 10 cm or 6 x 4 inches.)

Select decorations for the frame: flower petals, large buttons, pasta, foil bottle tops, stickers and/or glitter.

Activity

Show a couple of framed pictures of your own family to the children and let them ask any questions they may have. Ask about theirs. Say that today you're going to make a frame to keep a photo of their family in. Give each child a frame. Put their names on the back. Help them to decorate them with the glitter, stickers and crayons, etc.

Prayer

Invite them to hold up their frames.

Thank you for my family and all the people that I know. Amen.

TOP TIP

When finished, glue a magnet on the back so that the frame can be stuck to the fridge, or attach a piece of string to the back, so it can be hung on the wall.

Place mats

You will need: *A4 card; felt-tip pens or crayons; scissors; magazines/pictures of food; food wrappers and labels; glue sticks; snack.*

Preparation

Place the cards lengthways and write along the top of each a grace, such as the one below, or 'Thank you God for food, Amen.' From magazines, cut out several pictures of various foods for each child. You can also use food labels and wrappers with pictures.

Activity

When the children arrive, ask them to tell you their favourite foods. Show them the pictures and labels while asking if any of them like the food in the pictures. Tell them what kinds of foods you like too. Ask if any of them say thank you to God before they eat. Allow them time to tell you about any prayers they have at home. If they don't normally say grace, explain that you're going to make place mats together to remind them they can say thank you to God for the food they eat.

Show them the prepared pieces of card and read what it says: 'Thank you God for food. Amen.' Explain that they can glue pictures of food onto the cards to decorate them. Write their names on the backs of the card before they begin. Allow them some time to glue on pictures and colour the mats. Practise the prayer together a few times and then enjoy a snack.

Prayer

*For what we are about to receive
May the Lord make us truly thankful. Amen.*

> ### TOP TIP
> Laminate the place mats, so that they will be wipe-clean and permanent.

Play money

You will need: *Play money; real coins; purses; wallets; play tills; piggy bank/money box that can be opened easily.*

Preparation

Place all the coins in one pile. You can use foreign currency too.

Activity

Show the children the money and tell them the names of the coins. Point out different characteristics such as size, colour and weight. Allow them to handle the coins.

Ask the children if they have any money and where they keep it. Show them the purses, wallets and piggy banks/money boxes as possibilities. Ask what money is for. Show them the tills. Ask the children if they or their parents/carers ever buy anything. Let them play with the money, purses and tills. Invite them to sing an updated version of 'Jingle Bells' – 'Jingle coins, jingle coins, Jingle all the way, Oh what fun it is to sing a silly song today'.

Prayer

Invite the children to jingle the purses as you pray.

Thank you God for money and the things we can buy. Amen.

> ### TOP TIP
> You could introduce the idea of giving money in the church offering (Leviticus 27:30–33 and Deuteronomy 26:1–15). Show the children sample offering plates, bags or baskets and let them place change in them. Explain what the money is used for.

Safety note

Warn children not to put coins in their mouths and do not leave them unattended with coins around. Wash hands after playing with the money.

Please and thank you

You will need: No items needed.

Bible link

David's prayer of thanks: 1 Chronicles 16:7–36

Give thanks to the Lord: Psalm 136:1–9

Activity

Talk about what things we can say thank you to God for. David's psalms list lots of things he wanted to thank God for, for example, making the sun, moon and stars in the sky. Make a list but keep it very practical.

David also said thank you to God for helping him. Talk about some things that God can help us with, such as making us better when we're ill.

Incorporate the suggestions into the song below and sing to the tune of 'What shall we do with the drunken sailor?' Why not make up some actions to go with it?

Song

What do we say when we talk to Jesus,
What do we say when we talk to Jesus,
What do we say when we talk to Jesus,
Any time of day?

Thank you for the food we eat…

Thank you for the friends we play with…

Please help me when I start at school…

Prayer

Thank you God that you love it when we talk to you.

Praising

You will need: Child's microphone(s); tape recorder.

Bible link

Psalm for giving thanks: Psalm 100

Activity

Ask the children what we do with our voices? Let them practise using theirs. Invite them to whisper, 'Jesus loves you', shout, 'I love God', say their names normally and (if you're feeling brave) scream. Then ask them what makes them laugh. Try one of their suggestions to encourage them to laugh, such as tickling their toes. See who can laugh the most.

Introduce them to the microphone. Allow them to practise speaking into it and hearing their voices. Point out there is so much we can do with our voices: whisper, shout, talk, laugh, scream and even speak into a microphone. Explain that there was a man in the Bible called David. He loved to use his voice to sing and talk to God. Invite the children to join you in acting out a simple version of one of his songs. This song is a happy song that says 'thank you' to God.

Say the psalm through a few times. Remind the children that we can use our voices and actions to praise God. Also, just as we say and sing nice things to God, we can say nice things to our family and friends.

Prayer

Invite the children to join you in the actions.

Shout (Shout.) *to God!* (Point upwards.)
Yes, I (Point to oneself.) *love* (Fold arms across chest.)
God. (Point upwards.)
God (Point up.) *made me,* (Point to oneself.)
So I can walk (Walk.) *and run* (Run on the spot.)
and praise. (Wave your hands in the air.)
God is good. (Clap.)

Prayer cube

This activity is best suited to older pre-school children as the sticking can be quite fiddly.

You will need: *A3 thin card; template; scissors; glue sticks or sticky tape; felt-tip pens or crayons.*

Preparation

Photocopy and enlarge the template on the previous page onto thin card (one for each child). You may like to cut it out before giving it to the children.

Activity

Let children colour in the pictures. Then show them how to fold and stick the sides of the cube together – they will need lots of adult help with this.

Talk about the different pictures on the cube. They are all things we can enjoy and say thank you to God for.

Prayer

Get the children to practise rolling their prayer dice. What picture lands uppermost? Say a short prayer to thank God for whatever it is. Encourage the children to take their prayer cube home and use it there too.

TOP TIP

Instead of making individual prayer cubes, you could make one giant prayer cube for the group, taping six large squares of card together and sticking pictures on it. Encourage the children to take turns rolling it.

Prayer wheels

You will need: *Calendars; diaries; A4 card; split pin; felt-tip pens or crayons; glitter; stickers; glue or glue sticks; pair of compasses; protractor; pencils; scissors.*

Preparation

First make a template for the prayer wheels. Find the centre of a piece of A4 card by folding or find the point at which diagonals intersect. Place the point of your compasses on the centre of the card and set the distance at 9 or 9.5 cm. Draw and cut out the circle. Use this to cut all the others. (Alternatively find a tea plate with a diameter of between 10 and 20 cm and cut round that to make a template.)

Cut two card circles for each child. Using a protractor, divide one of each pair into 8 equal parts (the angle at the centre will be 45°), drawing in the divisions with a pencil. Leave one space for the child's name and write the days of the week in the other spaces. Cut out one eighth of the second circle and join together with the first at the centre with a split pin. The cutaway circle should be uppermost. This can be your demonstration wheel.

Activity

Ask the children if they know the names of the days of the week. Allow a few moments for answers and then encourage them to say them with you or repeat them after you. Show them some calendars and diaries of different sizes and styles and explain their use. Ask them on which days they can pray. You could point to different days in the calendar and diary and ask if they think they can pray on that day. Explain that God says we can pray on any day. Let them point to days on the calendars and diaries when they can pray.

Show your demonstration prayer wheel. As you turn to each new day, ask the children if they can pray on that day. Once again emphasise that they can talk to God on any day and at any time. Invite them to decorate their own prayer wheels. Encourage them to colour in all the days when they can pray to God. Assemble their wheels with the split pin and allow them to carry on colouring the wheel cover until everyone has finished. Make sure children do not hurt themselves with the split pins.

Prayer

Invite them to turn their wheels as you say the days.

Dear God, we thank you we can pray every day: Monday, Tuesday, Wednesday, Thursday, Friday, Saturday and Sunday. Amen.

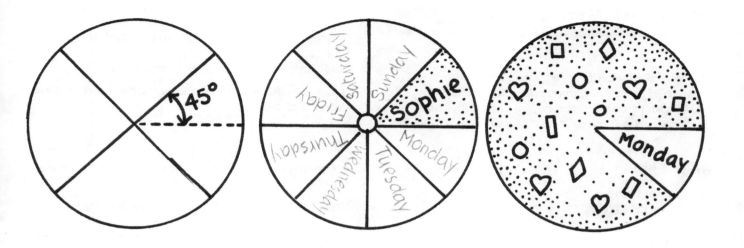

TOP TIP

You could write a letter to parents encouraging them to pray with their children on a certain day of the week for their friends in the group. The child could pray for a specific friend or the group in general.

Pretty faces

You will need: *Facilities for face-washing; kitchen roll; cotton wool pads; newspaper; paper plates and thick marker pen (optional); aprons; face paints; make-up applicators; assistant; mirror; Polaroid camera (optional).*

Bible link

I praise you because of the wonderful way you created me: Psalm 139:14 (CEV)

Preparation

If painting the children's faces, choose an area near the washing facilities. Put kitchen roll and cotton wool pads nearby to clean off the face paint. Put newspaper down to protect the floor. If you don't want to paint the children's faces, draw faces with thick marker on paper plates for children to decorate.

Activity

Ask the children if they've ever seen someone put on make-up or face paint. Allow them to tell you about it.

Ask if they'd like to put on some face paints. Explain that they must wear aprons to protect their clothes. Everyone can watch as you paint the children's faces. Alternatively, let the children put make-up and paint on the faces you've drawn on the paper plates.

Invite the children to look in the mirror and/or take a Polaroid photo.

Prayer

Invite them to hold up their photographs or paper-plate faces.

Thank you God for face paints and for making me.

> ### TOP TIP
> Invite a friendly clown to join the group.

Safety note

Check with parents and carers in advance if you are planning to use face paint as even those designed for children may provoke an allergic reaction in those with sensitive skins.

Puzzles

You will need: *Puzzles suitable for under-fives, including very simple lift-out types for toddlers.*

Preparation

Arrange the puzzles around the room making sure that the puzzle pieces are near the appropriate puzzle frame or the box lid is nearby.

Activity

Invite the children to look at one puzzle with you. Allow them to see the finished product and then break it up. Wait for suggestions, then partly remake the puzzle, but try placing one puzzle piece in all the wrong places. Each time, point out that it doesn't fit. When you find the right place, encourage everyone to clap. Point out that each puzzle piece is different and special and will only fit in once place. Remind them that they are all different and special too. Let them play with the puzzles.

Prayer

Encourage them to carefully bring the completed puzzles and place them near their feet.

Thank you God that all the puzzle pieces are different and special and so am I! Amen.

> ### TOP TIP
> You can tailor this activity to specific themes depending on the puzzles available.

Rainbow prayers

You will need: *Tissue paper in the following colours: red, orange, yellow, green, blue (light and dark), and purple; scissors; black sugar paper – one piece per child; glue sticks; cotton wool; picture of a rainbow.*

Bible link

The Flood: Genesis 6:5 – 9:17

Preparation

Cut the tissue paper into sections 5 cm square.

Activity

Ask the children if any of them have seen a rainbow. Did they think it was pretty? Show the picture. Explain that God showed Noah the rainbow so whenever Noah saw it, he could remember that God had promised never again to flood the earth again. Ask if they know the colours in the rainbow. Show them the tissue paper as a hint and encourage them to say the colours with you.

Invite them to make their own rainbows. First give them each a piece of black sugar paper to paste their rainbow on. Show them how to scrunch up the tissue paper and glue it to the card, then add the cotton wool as clouds. Remind them that when they look at their rainbow, they can remember that God always keeps his promises.

Prayer

Each child holds up their rainbow.

Dear God, thank you for colourful rainbows. Amen.

Prayer

Invite the children to hold up their sand jars.

Dear God, thank you for all the sand and beaches. Amen.

TOP TIP

If you live near the coast, how about arranging a trip to the beach? Children can collect their own sand and shells and you can use this activity to thank God for their mini-holiday.

Safety note

Make sure you get your sandpit sand from a reliable source. The best type to get is called silver sand (sometimes known as play sand), as other types may stain.

Sand jars

You will need: Beach holiday brochures and pictures; newspaper; beach items such as swimming costume, flip-flops, towel and sunglasses; beach toys; coloured sand; small jars with lids; old spoons; funnels; aprons; towel.

Preparation

Find pictures of holiday beaches (eg, from travel brochures). Try to include some with different coloured sands. If you have some pictures from your own holidays, use them. Spread newspaper on the table and the floor to make cleaning up simpler.

Activity

Explain that God created everything on the earth. Ask the children if they can think of things God created. Point out that God made the sea and beaches. Show children the beach pictures. Remind them that God made everything.

Ask if any of the children have been to the seaside. Let them talk about their holiday experiences. Ask what they took with them on holiday. Show them your beach things and let them handle the different items.

Remind the children of the different shades of sand in the pictures. Ask them which colour is their favourite. Show them the different colours of sand you have (if you are using artificially coloured sand, explain that there aren't beaches with these colours).

Tell the children to put on aprons so that they don't get sand on or in their clothes. Let them pretend to be at the seaside with the beach toys. (Use a sandpit if you have access to one.)

To conclude, invite them to collect some sand to take home with them. Use a spoon and funnel to get the sand into the jars. Screw the lids on tightly. Older children could layer different colours of sand. Use a towel to dust off any excess sand.

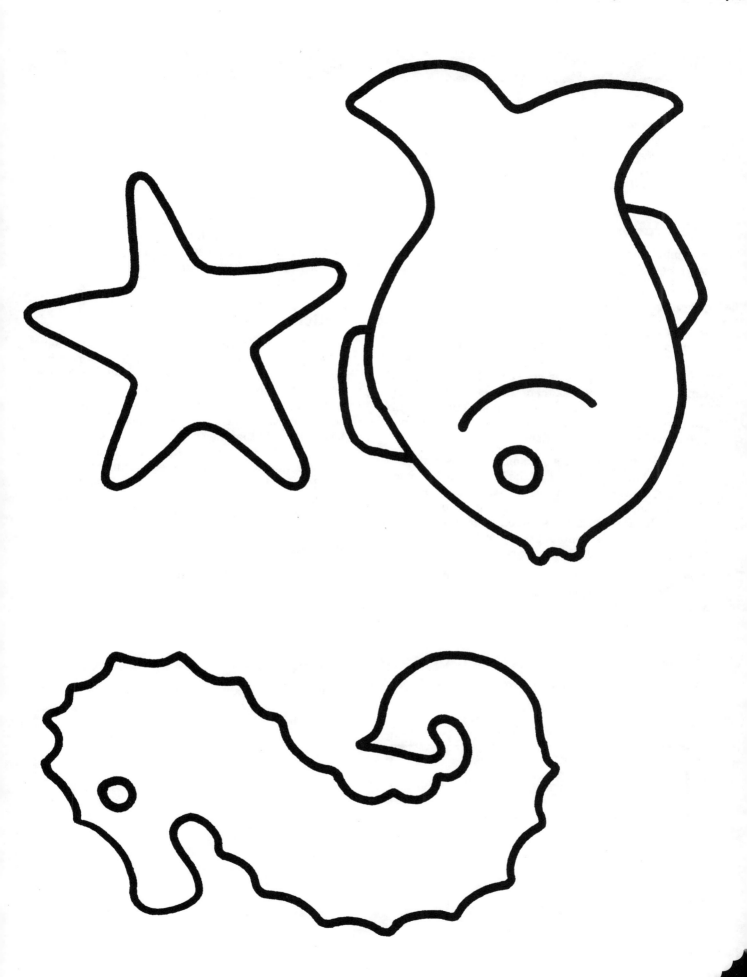

Sea creatures

You will need: *Pictures of sea creatures (template on previous page); small box for each child; felt-tip pens or crayons; play dough; play dough cutting and shaping tools; seaweed; pebbles; seashells; blue paper or paint and brushes; sand; scissors, glue; newspaper; aprons.*

Preparation

Assemble everything you will need for the activity. Put down newspaper to protect floors and tables.

Activity

Ask the children if they've ever been to the beach or seen the sea. Talk together about what colour the sea was and if they can remember seeing anything in the sea. If they suggest pebbles, seaweed and seashells, you can show them yours. Ask them what creatures live in the sea. Show the pictures as clues. Point out interesting features: the number of arms on a starfish and octopus, and the colours of tropical fish and coral.

Invite them to help make a sea home in a box. Put on aprons and make the inside of the box blue using blue paper or paint. Spread glue on the bottom and sprinkle on some sand. Then, using play dough or pictures, add fish, seashells, pebbles and seaweed. Admire their finished sea homes. Point out that just as we live in houses, these animals live in the sea.

Note: if your group is large, finding lots of boxes of the right size might be a problem. Instead of using boxes, you could create your seascape just as effectively on paper plates instead.

Prayer

Invite children to hold up their boxes (or paper plates).

Thank you God for the sea, and all the creatures that live there. Amen.

TOP TIP

Enjoy a trip to the aquarium or pet shop's fish department.

Sea shells

You will need: *Sea shells; pebbles; a non-transparent bag; newspaper; large bowl; small bowls; water; kitchen roll; plastic pots with lids.*

Preparation

Place some sea shells and pebbles in the bag and line up others along the side of the room, for the pretend walk on the beach. Put newspaper down to protect floor and tables. Fill all the bowls with water and place the kitchen roll nearby.

Activity

Show the children your bag. Invite them to put their hands in and try to guess what's inside. When everyone has had a turn, let each child take a shell or pebble out of the bag. Ask if they like sea shells and if anyone has walked along the beach to collect them? Invite them to collect and share the shells and pebbles on the pretend beach. Explain that they can play with their new pebbles and sea shells, feeling them in the bag, and placing them in water. Encourage them to see how different the pebbles look in the water and out of it. Finally the children could collect a few sea shells in a pot. Suggest they add water when they get home.

Prayer

Invite the children to hold up their sea shell pots.

Dear God, we thank you for making all kinds of pebbles and sea shells – flat ones, tiny ones, and big ones. And thank you for making me. Amen.

Safety note

Remember that young children can drown in just a few centimetres of water. NEVER leave children unattended near water.

Shapes

You will need: *A4 card (one sheet); scissors; square, triangular and circular items; basket; cheese and mini-cheeses from supermarket pick and mix selection (check for allergies); assorted cheese biscuits in different shapes; knife.*

Preparation

Cut out a square, triangle and circle from the A4 card. Collect items that match these shapes and put them into the basket. Cut the cheese into circles, triangles and squares.

Activity

Show the children your basket. Allow them time to handle the different items. Introduce them to the cut out shapes of square, triangle and circle. Point out the features of each: three sides, four sides and no sides – just round. Invite the children to help you sort out the items in the basket by shape. Finally, show them the snack. Say even snacks are in shapes. As you show them the mini-cheeses, cheese and crackers, ask them to name the shapes.

Prayer

Give each child a snack and get them to hold it up when that shape is mentioned.

Thank you God for all different shapes: squares, triangles and circles. Amen.

Shopping

You will need: *Clothes; food store items (either play or empty food boxes); toys; tills/cash registers; bags or baskets (non-polythene); scrap paper for 'shopping lists'.*

Preparation

Arrange the room like a shop, with a clothing, toy and food section. For the food section, you could use real food boxes and rinsed, empty bottles. Place a till or two near each section of the store.

Activity

Talk to the children about shopping. Invite them to talk about what they like and dislike about shopping. Ask if their parents/carers ever make a shopping list. Allow them to pretend to scribble a few items to buy on a shopping list.

Ask them if they've ever noticed the people who work in shops. Explain they are sometimes called sales assistants and they try to help shoppers. Then, invite them to go shopping. Encourage them to take turns being sales assistants. Invite them back together to show what they bought. Explain they'll need to tidy the shop and then the sales assistants can go shopping and the shoppers can be sales assistants.

Prayer

To close, invite them to hold up what they bought when you say it.

Dear God, thank you for shopping.
We can buy clothes, food and toys. Amen.

TOP TIP

Consider a trip to a nearby shop. Let the shopkeeper know in advance that you are coming.

Silent prayers

You will need: Baby dolls; timer; examples of items that make a noise such as a radio, phone, alarm clock, tool, scissors, clock that ticks, keyboard, food to stir, etc.

Bible link

Let all the world be silent – the Lord is present in his holy temple: Habakkuk 2:20 (CEV)

Activity

Talk about the difference between noisy and quiet. When is it good to be quiet? Let them make suggestions. Ask about ways to be quiet. Practise some of their ideas such as whispering, tiptoeing, sleeping. Ask what else makes quiet noises. If you have brought any of the items above, allow the children to listen and tell you if it's noisy or quiet. Remind them that God can hear all kinds of prayers including ones we whisper.

Create a few scenarios where they can practise being quiet such as tiptoeing to check on a sleeping baby (use the dolls); whispering when the baby wakes up; playing quietly when someone is sick; singing softly in the car or on public transport, and other ideas that you've discussed earlier. Allow them some free time playing very quietly.

Prayer

Show them the timer. Explain that you will set it for ten seconds and during that time, everyone will be as quiet as a mouse and say a quiet thank you to God for something they like. Close with a whispered prayer.

Thank you, God, that you can hear us even when we whisper. Amen.

> ### TOP TIP
> This is also an ideal prayer to practise quietly listening to God, possibly with some soft cushions and music.

Sky

You will need: Blue and black paper; cotton wool; yellow circles (for sun or moon); adhesive silver stars or silver milk bottle tops; glitter pens; felt-tip pens or crayons; glue sticks; pictures of the sky at night or during the daytime.

Preparation

Lay out the sheets of blue and black paper on tables with all the other bits and pieces with them.

Activity

Ask if the children have ever looked up into the sky. Let them tell you what they saw. As they do, show them the pictures you have brought. If possible, look outside to see some of the clouds and encourage their parents/carers to take them out at night and show them the stars.

Tell the children that today they will be making sky pictures. They can choose to do a picture of the sky at night-time or during the day. For the daytime sky, use the blue paper and encourage them to stick on the sun and the cotton wool for clouds and to draw on anything else that they might see in the sky – aeroplanes, etc. For a night sky, use the black paper and stick on a yellow moon and stars. Decorate with glitter pens if desired. Remind the children that God made the sky.

Prayer

Invite the children to hold up the corresponding pictures as you pray.

Thank you God for the sky with the sun and clouds in the day and the moon and stars in the night. Amen.

Stained-glass windows

You will need: Coloured plastic paper; scissors; pictures of stained-glass windows; OHP acetate with template from previous page copied onto it; glue sticks.

Preparation

Cut the plastic paper into rough shapes, approximately 5 cm in size.

Activity

Ask the children if they've ever seen glass in different colours. Explain that some churches have them as decorations and call them stained-glass windows. If your church has them, it would be nice to show them. You could also bring in a book with pictures of stained glass. Talk about what they think about the pictures or stained glass.

Explain that stained-glass windows in churches are like pictures in books. The coloured glass makes the light look coloured when it shines through. Show them some pieces of coloured plastic paper and let them see the different colours by holding it up to the light or a lamp. Encourage them to say the colours with you as they do it.

Invite the children to make their own coloured windows by gluing the coloured plastic onto the OHP acetates. When they've finished, admire their work and see if it tells a story.

Prayer

Invite the children to hold their stained-glass windows up to the light.

Dear God, thank you for light,
and the colours in the windows. Amen.

> ### TOP TIP
> You can adapt this activity to reinforce another theme by changing the image in the stained-glass window to stars, shapes, rainbows, colours or an idea of your own.

Story time

You will need: Bible; children's Bible; assorted books.

Preparation

The week before, ask if the children have Bibles and favourite stories at home. If so, encourage them to bring them in the following week. Make sure parents/carers know.

Activity

Talk to the children about their favourite stories and read one or two. See how many of the children have a special book called the Bible at home. Explain it's a special storybook that helps us learn about God. Read a couple of stories from the children's Bible.

Prayer

Encourage all the children to place their hands on the Bible as you pray.

Dear God, we thank you for all that we can learn in the Bible.
Help us and our friends to learn about you when we read it. Amen.

Surprises

You will need: Small cloth or paper bags; marbles; flower petals; buttons; wrapped sweets; bobbins; dried pasta; small toys; crayons; shredded paper.

Preparation

Place each set of items in a separate, non-transparent bag. Substitute other child-friendly items, depending on what you have available. Remember which bag has the sweets in.

Activity

Ask the children if they like surprises. Explain you have some bags with things in, but you're not quite sure what is in each bag. Ask if they'd like to put their hands in the different bags and see if they can guess what's inside. Get parents/carers/assistants to help by holding some of the bags. Encourage the children to feel inside the bag, without peeping or removing items. Let everyone who wants to, have a turn.

Come back together to reveal what is in each bag. Allow a different child each time to come up, feel inside the bag, share his or her guess with the group and then pull out some of the contents. Encourage them to be surprised and laugh if wrong. Save the sweets till last.

Prayer

Invite children to hold up one of the surprises they liked best and say:

Thank you God. Surprises are fun! Amen.

> ## TOP TIP
> Invite them to play a game of hide-and-seek.

Telephones

You will need: Telephones (assorted sizes and styles); toy mobile phones; paper cups; string.

Preparation

If you do not have enough telephones to go round, make them using paper cups and string.

Activity

Show children the telephones. What are they for? Have they ever talked on the phone? Who have they talked to? Let them play with the phones and mobiles. After a few minutes, ask who they were talking to and what they were talking about. Remind them that when we talk on the phone, we can't see the other person but they can hear us and we can hear them. Just as when we talk to God, we can't see him, but he can hear us. Allow them some further free time, encouraging them to pretend to phone each other and even talk to God.

Prayer

Sing *'Prayer is like a telephone'* (ks 286)

Toy box

Many churches support overseas charities by collecting toys or sending filled shoeboxes. There may be organisations or charities nearer home which would also benefit from good quality toys for which you have no further use.

You will need: Toys; wrapping paper (glitter, crêpe or festive); scissors; sheet of paper for label; large packing case; glue sticks; felt-tip pens or crayons.

Preparation

The week before, explain to the children that you are going to collect toys to send to children who don't have many, and that the following week you will need their help decorating the box that the toys will be sent in. Cut the wrapping paper into A5-sized pieces. Make a sign for the box stating who the collection is for.

Activity

Allow the children some free play with toys. When they have finished, ask them to help you put them away in the toy box. As you gather together, ask if they had fun and what their favourite toy is. Explain that some children don't have many toys, so we're going to help by sending them a toy box. Remind them that their parents/carers may have brought some toys to donate or explain that other people will be bringing toys to give to these children.

Show the children the coloured paper. Say you would like them to help you decorate the toy box by gluing the wrapping paper onto the box and colouring any bare spots. Give them time to decorate the box. When it's finished, encourage them to put any gifts inside the box. Explain that the children who receive them will say thank you for letting them have some toys too. Leave the box in a prominent place when the building is in use, but keep it somewhere safe at other times.

Prayer

Encourage the children to place their hands on the box as you pray for the children who will receive the toys.

Dear God, thank you for our toys.
We hope the children will like playing with these. Amen.

Traceable bodies

You will need: Large rolls of paper (eg, lining paper) or A1 card (2 pieces per child); sticky tape; scissors; assistant; felt-tip pens or crayons; fruit or vegetable snack.

Bible link

The body is the temple of the Holy Spirit: 1 Corinthians 3:16–17

Preparation

If using A1 card, tape two pieces together for each child. If using lining paper, cut pieces roughly the height of the children. Label the top of the card or roll 'Thank you God for making me'.

Activity

Explain that God made our bodies and that he thinks our bodies are important. What can we do to take care of our bodies? Repeat together any actions that they suggest. For example, pretend to wash your hair, go to sleep, exercise, eat vegetables and so on. Other possibilities include a simple aerobics activity or dance routine followed by a healthy snack of fruit and/or vegetables.

Next explain that you are going to trace round the children. Let each child lie down and with assistance trace round the outline of their body. Let them colour and decorate the body shape, adding various features. While the children are colouring, tell them the caption says: 'Thank you God for making me'.

Prayer

Invite the children to place a hand on their outline.

Dear God, we thank you that you've made us.
Help us to look after the bodies you've given us. Amen.

Uniforms

You will need: *A variety of uniforms (real or child's versions) such as white coats for doctors; fireman's helmet; policeman's hat; hard hat; fluorescent jacket for street cleaners; chainstore uniforms; business suits; relevant toys: a doctor's kit; tool kit; toy tills, etc.*

Preparation

Assemble uniforms and toys.

Activity

Ask the children to name some of the jobs that people do. Encourage them to think of doctors, teachers, police officers, the people who help us in shops, office workers etc. As they mention each job, talk about what those people do to help us.

Show the children the uniforms and see if they know who might wear them. Point out some of the differences in colour and style. Allow them some free play trying on the various uniforms and using the appropriate toys for that particular job.

Prayer

While the children are still dressed up, come together to pray. Invite them to stand up when you give thanks for their job. You could practise once, so that they know when to stand.

Dear God, we thank you for all the different jobs people do:
doctor, policeman, nurse, fireman, builder, street cleaner, shop worker.
Thank you for their help. Amen.

> **TOP TIP**
> Invite some friendly professionals to come, dressed in their uniform, and talk about their job.

Wakey, wakey

You will need: *Sleeping or camping mats; blankets (optional); hairbrushes; toothbrushes; toast; alarm clock.*

Preparation

Gather all of the objects together for the children to use.

Activity

Welcome the children. Ask them what wakes them up in the mornings. When they woke up this morning were they sleepy, grumpy or wide awake? See what they do when they wake up. If necessary, offer suggestions like brushing their hair and teeth, getting dressed, eating breakfast and so on. Ask if they would like to show you what they do when they get up. Invite them to lie down on the mats and pretend to sleep. Explain that you're going to set the alarm and go to sleep too. When the alarm goes off, you can all get up.

Let the alarm go off one minute later. Encourage the children to say, 'Good morning' to each other. Ask them how they feel. To wake up, do a few big stretches to the sky and to their toes. Then it's time to get dressed. But first they must pretend to take off their nightclothes. Then, pretend to put on a vest/T-shirt/shirt, trousers, socks and shoes. Walk to the bathroom and pretend to brush your hair.

Then go to the kitchen for toast. You could serve toast squares with Marmite or jam as the snack. (Avoid peanut butter because of allergies.) After 'breakfast' it's time to brush our teeth. Then we can play.

Prayer

Invite them to close with a rhyme, following your actions.

Thank you for sleep, (Rest hand on shoulders.)
Thank you for being awake, (Stretch upwards.)
We put on our clothes, (Put on a pretend top and trousers.)
We clean our teeth, (Pretend to brush teeth.)
Now we're really awake! (Jump up.) *Amen!*

Walls of Jericho

You will need: Building blocks (or boxes taped together)

Bible link

The fall of Jericho: Joshua 6

Activity

Invite the children to help you build a wall with the boxes. When you've finished, look puzzled. Ask them how they think you could get through a wall like this. (A quick child may try to knock it over or create a door for you. If so, rebuild and ask them not to knock it over yet.) Explain that there was a city in the Bible with very strong walls and that God's people were outside the city. They couldn't get in because the walls were so strong, but God told them he would help them. Guess what God told them to do? He told them to walk all round the outside of the wall once.

Invite the children to walk round singing a song such as 'My God is so big'. After marching, stop and look at the wall. Point out that it still hasn't fallen over. So suggest walking round again like the people in the Bible. Explain that God told the people to walk round the city six times, once a day. On the seventh day they marched around it seven times and then blew trumpets and gave a great big shout! Invite the children to march around it seven times with you and shout loudly at the end. Then the big walls fell over and God's people could go inside. Invite them to knock the walls over and walk through the debris.

Prayer

On the other side of the wall, or in amongst the boxes, have a little quiet huddle and sing:

'*My God is so big*', (ks 255)

Walking in the sand

You will need: Newspaper; small sandpit with sand; sand toys; two towels; sandpit cover; flip-flops in small sizes.

Preparation

Place newspaper on the floor. Place the sandpit in the centre of it. Lay a towel on top of the newspaper at one end of the sandpit. Leave the second towel folded on top of the first. Ensure the floor is clean.

Activity

Ask the children how good they are at walking. Let them practise. Encourage them to try jogging, jumping and skipping too. Invite the children to take their shoes and socks off. Explain that in a few moments, they'll see how different it feels to walk in bare feet. Let them practise walking and moving about barefoot. See how easy or difficult the children think it was.

Uncover the sandpit and point out the sand. Explain that they will each get a turn to see what it is like to walk on the sand. Allow them each a turn, starting from the end opposite the towels. Afterwards, ask them how it felt. Was it easy? Try a second trip through wearing flip-flops. Ask them if that was easier or more difficult. If your sandpit is big enough, allow them to walk in it together. Finally, allow them some free play in the sand with some sand toys.

When they get to the end with the towels, let them stand on the one towel and use the folded towel to wipe the sand from their feet. When everyone has had a turn, cover the sandpit.

Prayer

Dear God, we thank you for our feet
and all the walking we can do with them, even on sand.
Amen.

Watch a clock

You will need: Paper plates; card; scissors; split pin; watches; clocks (including different sorts of alarm clocks); felt-tip pens or crayons; clip art pictures: breakfast, sandwich, cooked meal, sleeping child, toy; glue sticks.

Preparation

To make a clock, cut two strips of card for the hands. Attach them to the paper plate using split pin. Put some tape over the sharp ends of the pin.

Activity

Show your watches and clocks. See if any of the children have their own watch on. Invite the children to gently try the watches on and hold the clocks. Ask what watches and clocks are for. Allow them to tell you about clocks they have at home and if they make any sounds like ticking and chiming. You can practise the sounds with the children using a rhythm of tick-tock, tick-tock, dong. Invite them to see what happens when you set the alarms. Wait a moment and then let the alarms go off. Ask them which alarm they like best: radio, buzzer or bell.

Explain that clocks and watches help us know what time it is – such as breakfast time, lunchtime, dinner time, bedtime, nap time and playtime. Let the children tell you which time they like best.

Ask them if they'd like to make their own clocks and add the times of the day using the clip art pictures instead of numbers. Give out a paper plate and a set of pictures to each child. Put their names on the back before they begin. Help them glue the clip art pictures to the clocks. Allow them some time to colour their clocks and move the hands. Remind them that we can talk to God at all times because he's always there.

Prayer

Invite them to turn their clock hands as you pray:

Dear God, thank you that you're with us all the time: playtime, breakfast time, lunchtime and dinner time, and bedtime. Amen.

Safety note

Be careful. Split pins have sharp ends!

We are family

You will need: *Sheet of poster card or sugar paper; thick marker pens; small paper plates (dessert size); wool; scissors; two buttons per child; one plastic bottle top per child; small twigs; glue sticks.*

Preparation

Label a large sheet of poster card or sugar paper: 'We are (*insert group name*).' Cut the wool into various lengths. Create a sample face with your own hair- and eye-colouring using the buttons as eyes, the bottle top as a nose and a twig as a mouth. Lastly, add some coloured wool as hair. You may wish to use stickers or coloured reinforcements for facial features, as young children will be tempted to put buttons in their mouths.

Activity

Explain and/or remind the children that their group has a special name. Tell them the name and explain who can be part of their group. Give the children time to say what they like about the group and what they would like to do more.

Invite them to help you make a special poster of the group to go on display. Show them the poster card and read what it says. Explain that they are each going to make a picture of themselves, then show them the picture you've made of yourself. Help them to glue and decorate their own pictures. Lastly, invite them to glue their plates to the big poster.

Prayer

If possible and practical, go to the place where the poster will be displayed. Otherwise, just hold the poster up. Explain that you want to thank God for everyone in the group and when you say their names, they can touch their faces on the poster. For larger groups, say several children's names at a time.

Dear God, we thank you for our group.
Thank you for (insert name), (insert name), and (insert name).
Thank you we can play and learn about God. Amen.

Safety note

As with any public place we do not have control over who visits the premises. For child protection reasons, it is inadvisable to display photographs and names of children in a public area.

Weather prayers

You will need: *Pictures of various types of weather; umbrella; wellies; raincoats; winter coats; hats; gloves; scarves; snowsuit; snow boots; shovel; shorts and T shirts; sunglasses; flip-flops; baseball cap; spring/autumn coat.*

Preparation

Gather all the objects together, close to you.

Activity

Ask the children about their favourite type of weather. Tell them yours. Go through the seasons, focusing on what it feels like in that season. For example, winter is cold but in summer it is warm. In spring, it rains a lot and in the autumn it can be quite windy. Let them say which season they like best.

Ask what types of clothes and shoes they should wear in the different types of weather. Do they need anything else like umbrellas, sunglasses, hats and so on? As they answer, show them the different articles you have brought. Invite them to show you what they would be doing in each type of weather, perhaps using the items you've shown them. For example, they could be making snowmen, playing at the beach, going for a walk in the park, and collecting leaves. Give them some time to dress up and pretend to do the activities related to each type of weather.

Prayer

Invite the children to stand in a circle, still in weather costume. As you thank God for each type of weather, ask the children wearing that costume to step into the centre of the circle and clap. Explain that at the end you'll thank God for all types of weather and everyone can come to the centre and clap.

Dear God, we thank you for winter and snow.
Thank you for spring and the rain,
And the summer and the hot sun.
Thank you for autumn and the pretty leaves.
Thank you for all types of weather. Amen.

Weddings

You will need: *Photographs of a wedding; flowers (real or artificial); dressing-up clothing; piece of lace or a veil; hats; confetti.*

Bible links

Jesus turns water into wine: John 2:1–11

Parable of the wedding banquet: Matthew 22:1–14

Wedding of the Lamb: Revelation 19:6–9

Activity

Show the children some photographs of weddings: either personal ones or ones from a wedding magazine. Ask if any of the children have ever been to a wedding. See whose wedding they attended and what they wore. Let them tell you if they had a special role at the wedding. Explain that you're going to have a pretend wedding, so you need everyone's help.

Give the children the different costumes: flowers and dresses for the bride and bridesmaids, hats for the groom and groomsmen, and a veil for the bride. Give them brief instructions about walking down the aisle. Let them practise a few times with a little guidance from you.

Stage the pretend wedding. You could do this more than once so that everyone has a chance to wear the bride and groom costumes. Explain that weddings are special days for the bride and the groom and their family and friends. People come and bring them presents and wish them lots of happiness as a new family.

Prayer

Invite them to throw confetti in the air when you say, 'Amen'.

Thank you God for weddings and for all the new families. Amen!

Wet feet

You will need: *Bowls; water; towels; flannels; jugs; funnels; bath toys; paddling pool (optional); bathing costumes (optional); aprons; perfume (optional).*

Bible links

Jesus anointed by a sinful woman: Luke 7:36–50

Mary anoints Jesus' feet: John 12:1–3

Jesus washes his disciples' feet: John 13:1–17

Preparation

Fill the bowls/pool with warm water. Place the bowls on the towels with funnels, jugs and bath toys nearby.

Activity

Explain that back in Bible times, they didn't have roads like ours. People used to walk along dirt roads and their feet got very sandy and muddy. They had baths and wore sandals, but they didn't have socks like we do so their feet got very dusty. Explain that one night before dinner, Jesus was sitting with his friends. They had walked a lot that day and they had very dirty feet. They were quite smelly. (*Invite children to hold their noses with you.*) Nobody really wanted to wash people's feet, because they were dirty and smelly. But Jesus got up and washed everyone's feet as he told them he loved them. Stress that people then had very dirty feet and that washing other people's feet wasn't a very nice job, but Jesus did it because he loved them!

Alternatively, explain there was once a woman named Mary and another woman whose name we don't know. Because they loved Jesus so much, they washed his feet with perfume. Let them smell the perfume you've brought. Explain that today our feet don't get so dirty because we wear shoes and socks, but we do get fluff between our toes. Wash their feet. You could encourage them to wear aprons and wash each other's feet in pairs. Include parents and carers.

Explain that we can do things for other people too. They can help others get washed and clean – such as their little brothers and sisters or their friends. They can also help others by doing jobs they don't always want to do, like tidying their toys. Allow them some free time playing with the water and toys.

Prayer

Invite them to put their hands in the water.

Dear God, we thank you that Jesus did good things for people.
Help us to help other people too. Amen.

When I hurt myself

You will need: *Dolls; teddy bears; plasters and bandages; doctors and nurses toys: stethoscopes, toy first aid kits, etc.*

Activity

Ask if any of the children have ever hurt themselves. Invite them to tell you about it. Some may have scars they can show the group. Ask what happened after they hurt themselves. Did someone make it better by sticking a plaster on it? Did they go to the doctor or even the hospital? What was it like?

Show them some dolls and bears. Explain that they have all hurt themselves and need someone to look after them. Ask if the children would like to do this. Set up a pretend doctor's surgery and hospital. Allow them some free time taking care of the dolls and teddy bears. Be sure to ask what ailments and injuries the dolls and bears are suffering from and how the children are going to help make it better.

Talk about any people you know in the group or any friends or relatives of the children who may be unwell. Say you're going to pray for them now.

Prayer

Thank you God that you care when we're poorly; please help (name) to get well soon. Amen

Training feature

Play with a purpose

Watching young children play is fascinating. The cries of delight as children make discoveries, pleas of, 'Watch me!' or, 'Look what I've made!' usually produce a positive adult response.

So, what should our three- and four-year-olds be 'doing' when we meet with them in our groups? Learning about God? Yes, of course. But perhaps we need to ask ourselves a few more searching questions:

- Do we think young children can learn about a creator God?

- Do we think it is important for children to be creative – just like their heavenly Father?

- Do we think they could or should express their capacity to be creative in a church setting?

Creative play is the means by which a child can think, imagine, express, make connections, develop and manipulate materials in a deeply satisfying and rewarding way. If we present children with the right opportunities, play and creativity can go hand in hand.

What does God think about play and creativity?

God likes creativity. His creation displays the glory of God. The activity of human creativity can be seen to mirror the activities of our creator God – we are made in his image. How wonderful that we can be creative just like God himself.

Why do children need to play?

Any session for three- and four-year-olds which is too prescriptive can drive out the desire, time, energy – and ability – of the young child in their attempt to be creative as God is creative.

You can learn so much about the way children think, learn and understand the world by observing their play. There is no doubt that play has a particular function from the way it acts as a vehicle for all sorts of learning. Play and creativity is all about taking risks; it's about being different and individual, and the young child needs to feel safe and secure enough to take those risks. Being creative and playing is also about thinking for yourself; taking responsibility, making decisions about what might and might not work, rehearsing skills and persevering through difficulties encountered. Certainly,

it can't be true to say that a child 'is just playing' when so much is going on!

With your team, other children's workers or a friend:

- discuss together the ways in which humans differ from animals.

- think further about the human capacity to be creative.

- consider how church life can enhance our God-given creative abilities and gifts.

Play presents many opportunities

Play provides the child with opportunities to use and explore what they know about the world, God and others in a way that will help them 'get to grips' with this knowledge. When a child is engaged in play, they are able to think about what they know, reflect on experiences and come to terms with their emotions, feelings and relationships. All this is crucial for the development of a positive self-image. Play experts tend to avoid a definition of play and find it more useful to describe its features. These open up a world of opportunities for the young child as they:

- develop successful relationships with others, for example, learning to take turns when sharing materials such as crayons or paint.

- gain control over their emotions, learning to negotiate turns using a favourite piece of equipment to act out a Bible story.

- explore their environment and make discoveries, in activities such as manipulating natural materials like shells.

- create individual work by using musical instruments to compose own songs about God.

- gain confidence in their physical skills, perhaps by using a range of drawing equipment to express how they feel about God's love for them.

- gain confidence in their intellectual skills, develop concentration, curiosity and imagination through sensitive adult interaction.

- imitate others and learn from them by watching how other children treat each other whilst engaged in role play using props.

- act out troubling situations in a safe way, by using small play-people, dolls or toys.

- explore solutions to problems in life, perhaps using puppets to enact possible answers.

With your team, other children's workers or a friend:

- talk together about the last time you watched a child playing.

- describe what skills they were using.

- think together about why the child was playing and what you think the child gained by playing.

What is 'quality play' really about?

Quality play is extremely positive because it's all about what a child can do, not what they can't do! Quality play provides children with greater opportunities to learn and it is essential to allow time for such play so that they can learn! They need first-hand experiences which allow them to explore the world, make discoveries and practise their skills. Children can realise their experiences in a range of ways, for example, composing music, dancing, drawing, painting or modelling.

Adults in church settings have an important role in facilitating quality play. A shift in priorities doesn't necessarily mean extra work, just rearranging what we choose to do in our short and limited time with them.

What do children need to play and be creative?

Allowing time for children to be creative and play doesn't mean that we scrap our prepared material! We need to change the way we treat the time and materials. Children do need to learn the biblical stories and, as the Bible says, a solid knowledge of the word of God will guide them all through life. This might mean allowing time after you have told the Bible story to explore what you are learning in a child-led way. This is not where anarchy begins! The adult still needs to be in control. Rather than dictating exactly how the children should interpret or express their understanding of the Bible, new ways can be developed to help children come to terms with what they are hearing and learning, and apply it to their own life in a way that is meaningful to them. It's really about providing the time and resources to allow this to happen.

Help! We haven't got the resources or finances!

The good news is that provision for play need not be expensive. It may mean asking friends and neighbours to help contribute suitable materials but people are usually keen to contribute things they may well have thrown away anyway! Larger items like sand and water will require an initial outlay, but often these items can be picked up second hand. Car boot sales are a never-ending supply of useful materials for play and are so cheap! You

may also be able to get your group registered with an Educational Supplier. You will then be able to pick up items which would be too expensive in the shops.

You will need a plastic sheet to cover the floor and a dustpan and brush for sweeping up the sand (encourage the children to help with this task at the end of the session). Storage needs to be considered but often there will be someone in your church who has a suitable place – ask! Otherwise the spare room, back of the garage or shelf in the cupboard at home may be needed, but it is worth it! Once the materials are in place, and being gathered on a weekly basis, preparation time will be reduced and the best bonus of all will be that the children will come to look forward to their time with you. Children really enjoy being creative and find it totally absorbing. You won't need to worry about what to do with the children next time the sermon runs on!

Here is a list of basic material to get quality play and creativity under way:

Cardboard boxes – any shape or size
Egg boxes
Adhesive (paste, PVA, sticks)
Adhesive tape
Crayons
Pencils
Child-safe scissors (remember to have some left-handed ones)
Paint
'Fuzzy felt'
Books
Collage materials
Natural materials, eg, shells, sponges
Large sheets of paper
Newspaper to cover tables
Shiny materials (paper or anything shiny!)
Modelling clay
Clay (buying in bulk is much cheaper)
Paper-towel rolls
Old musical instruments
Scrap books
Old magazines
Chenille wire (pipe cleaners!)
Role-play clothes: hats, gloves, masks, long gowns, etc (Avoid high heels as they can be dangerous. Make sure the gowns are not too long so as to cause children to trip.)
Materials for printing, eg, sponges
Puppets

What can the children do with all these materials?

You need to consider the structure of your session. Perhaps the children can play for a short time before you tell them a Bible story, or maybe it would be more appropriate to wait until after the story. Then, ask the children to tell you what they thought, what were the best bits, how did they feel about the story? Explain that the children will be playing with the materials you have brought in with you today. If you have used puppets (probably ones you have made yourself) to tell the story, one or two children will love to re-enact it. That way they will know the story inside out. If you have a large group and enough adult helpers, it might be best to rotate some of the activities, but with smaller groups they can all work with the same materials. You need to decide in advance how this part of the session will work practically.

Children need to know the boundaries

Be very clear with the children what you expect of them when they play with others, share materials, take turns, etc. Remind them of the rules when necessary, for example, you must insist on 'no throwing sand'. Children appreciate being told the rules in advance!

Organising play with a mixed age range

If you have a mixed age group you will need to think carefully about which activities are appropriate to all ages. Above all else, the children must be safe. You could consider how the older children could help the younger ones with activities. Of course, with extra help, it's easier to meet all their needs – perhaps you could ask for an extra assistant to come and help you at this point in your session.

Keep talking (and listening)

You can make suggestions on how to play with the materials you have laid out but be careful not to suggest that this is the only way they can play (their ideas are bound to be better). Once the activity is under way, talk to the children individually about what they are doing – use open-ended questions so they don't have to say something just to please you! As you go round talking to the children, share your experiences of God with them. For instance, you may have just told the children the story of the feeding of the five thousand. You could tell them about a time you felt hungry and realised you didn't have anything in the cupboard when a friend came round with a lovely cake they had just made. Your experience may not be about feeding the five thousand but it's the sort of situation young children can easily relate to. Children will then offer their own experiences. Together you can say how good God is every day. Perhaps, as you sit next to the children, you too could make a cake out of modelling clay. Children love adults to play alongside them and it promotes quality conversation and helps reduce negative behaviour.

Role-play facilitates understanding

Role-play is an effective way of helping children understand more fully the story they have just heard.

Acting out the parts, with your direction if necessary, is great fun and brings home the reality of the Bible story. For example, you may choose to help the children act out the story of Zacchaeus and the children could pretend to climb a tree to see Jesus as you talk them through the story again. Children (and other adults) find this great fun, particularly if you add some humour to it!

They might not have anything to take home with them!

It doesn't matter! The 'doing' of the activity is the important part, and sometimes that will mean there is nothing to show for it. Just remember that a huge amount may well have been accomplished. We want our young children to take home their understanding of how much God loves them. He thinks they are terrific and, if that is achieved by role-playing a scene from a Bible story, then that's fine!

Keep safe

Any play with water must be carefully supervised as children can drown in a very small amount of water. If you have a large group, one adult must be assigned to this activity alone. Of course, if you have a small group all playing with water, you can supervise the activity yourself. However, if one child needs individual attention for any reason, you must be able to call on extra help or you will have to stop all the children playing while you sort out the situation.

Be careful to look over all the materials you are going to offer the children. Are there any sharp edges? Could they swallow anything? Is the material toxic? If you are eating or drinking, do any of the children in your group suffer from allergies? Role-play clothes must be clean and not cause children to trip over.

Negative and all unwanted behaviour must be dealt with firmly but kindly – free play is not a licence for children to hurt others or interrupt their play.

Keep busy

Free play is not free time for adult leaders! You must take an active role in these areas:

• plan exciting play activities each week.

• provide suitable, safe playthings.

• set up the room or space you have been given.

• intervene in any disputes, encouraging the children to share resources when necessary.

• maintain a presence with all the children so that they know you are interested in what they are doing and that rules must not be broken.

• clear up afterwards (although the children should be involved in clearing away as much as possible).

Keep happy

Be enthusiastic about the activities and whatever the children produce. Tell the children how great they are and that God thinks they are wonderful. Be positive as much as you can, as often as you can. You will probably never know just how much your encouraging words have meant to them. Play away!

About the author
Jackie Harding (MA in Christian Education) was a lecturer in early years and childcare before taking up headship of a primary school. She is an established author of several books about childcare, education and play and has published several books for children. Presently, she works as an early years consultant, primarily for the Department for Education and Skills (DfES).

Bibliography

Helping Young Children to Develop by Jackie Harding & Liz Meldon-Smith (Hodder & Stoughton, 1999, ISBN 0-340-72078-6)

How to make Observations and Assessments by Jackie Harding & Liz Meldon-Smith (Hodder & Stoughton, 1996 ISBN 0-340-64748-5)

Play in early childhood, from birth to six years by Mary Sheridan, revised and updated by Jackie Harding & Liz Meldon-Smith (Routledge 1999, ISBN 0-415-18693-5)

Appendix A

Stocking a supply cupboard

Aprons or old shirts which completely cover clothing

Bowls (assorted sizes)

Broom

Bucket and cleaning materials

Card: A1 or A2, A4

Clip art book

Coloured material – assorted scraps

Coloured marker pens, pens, pencils, or crayons

Construction or coloured photocopy paper

Dustpan and brush

Glitter

Glue sticks or PVA glue and spreaders

Handwash

Hole punch

Short smooth sticks

Kitchen roll

Large roll of paper (wall lining paper or fax paper rolls)

Old magazines

Newspaper

Paint

Paintbrushes

Paper plates – assorted sizes

Post-it notes

Poster card

Scissors

Small boxes

Split pins (paper fasteners)

Stickers

Sticky tape

String

Sugar paper

Tissue paper

Wrapping paper

Wool or elastic

Small vacuum cleaner

Appendix B

Bible references and related prayer activities

Old Testament

Genesis 1–2	Creation	Creating creation
Genesis 6:5 – 9:17	The flood	Fun with play dough
		Noah's ark
		Rainbow prayers
Genesis 15:5,6	God's covenant with Abram	God keeps his promises
Genesis 21	Birth of Isaac	God keeps his promises
		Baby, baby
Genesis 37	Story of Joseph	Coat of many colours
Exodus 2:1–10	Birth of Moses	Baby, baby
Exodus 19	At Mount Sinai	Mountains and hills
Exodus 25:10–22	The Ark (God's special box)	God's special box
Leviticus 23:33–44	The Festival of Shelters	Festival of Shelters
Leviticus 27:30–33	Tithe	Play money
Deuteronomy 26:1–15	First-fruits and tithes	Play money
Joshua 6	Fall of Jericho	Walls of Jericho
Ruth 1–4	Ruth and Naomi	Moving house

1 Samuel 1	Birth of Samuel	Baby, baby
1 Samuel 16:11	David the shepherd	Baa, baa
1 Samuel 20	David and Jonathan	Friendship bracelets
1 Kings 17:1–6	Elijah	Birds
1 Chronicles 16:7–36	David's psalm of thanks	Please and thank you
Psalm 20:5	Shout for joy... Lift up our banners	Banners, singing and praise
Psalm 23	The Lord is my shepherd	Baa, baa
Psalm 43:5	I will yet praise him	Musical praise
Psalm 63:4	I will praise you	Musical praise
Psalm 91:11 (GNB)	God will put his angels in charge	Angels
Psalm 95:7	We are his sheep	Baa, baa
Psalm 100	Psalm for giving thanks	Praising
Psalm 136:1–6	Give thanks to the Lord	Please and thank you
Psalm 139:13–14	Fearfully and wonderfully made	Pretty faces
		Mixed feelings
Proverbs 17:17	A friend loves at all times	Friendship bracelets
Habakkuk 2:20 (CEV)	Let all the world be silent – the Lord is present in his holy temple	Silent prayers

New Testament

Matthew 1:18–25	Birth of Jesus Christ	Baby, baby
Matthew 13:1–43	Parable of the sower	Growing seeds
Matthew 14:13–21	Jesus feeds the five thousand	Bread
		Fishy fish
Matthew 22:1–14	Parable of the wedding banquet	Weddings
Matthew 22:34–40	The greatest commandment	Hearts
Matthew 26:17–30	The Last Supper	Bread
Mark 1:17	Jesus calls the first disciples to be fishers of men	Fishing
Mark 6:30–44	Jesus feeds the five thousand	Bread
		Fishy fish
Mark 10:46–52	Blind Bartimaeus receives his sight	Glasses
Mark 14:12–26	The Last Supper	Bread
Luke 2:1–20	Birth of Jesus Christ	Baby, baby
Luke 5:4	Jesus calls Simon Peter	Fishing
Luke 7:36–50	Jesus anointed by a sinful woman	Wet feet
Luke 8:1–15	Parable of the sower	Growing seeds
Luke 9:10–17	Jesus feeds the five thousand	Bread
		Fishy Fish
Luke 12:7	The hairs of your head are numbered	God loves me
Luke 22:7–20	The Last Supper	Bread
John 1:4–5	Jesus is the Light	Let your light shine
John 2:1–11	Jesus turns water into wine	Weddings
John 3:16–21	For God so loved the world	Hearts
John 6:1–15	Jesus feeds the five thousand	Bread
		Fishy Fish
John 9:1–41	Jesus heals a man born blind	Glasses
John 10:1–18	Jesus is the Good Shepherd	Baa, baa
John 12:1–4	Mary anoints Jesus' feet	Wet feet
John 13:1–17	Jesus washes his disciples' feet	Wet feet
John 13:34	A new commandment	Hearts
John 15:13	Lay down one's life for one's friends	Friendship bracelets
John 17:6–19	Jesus prays for his disciples	Model churches
John 21:1–14	Jesus appears to the disciples after his resurrection	Fishing
Romans 15:11	Praise the Lord	Musical praise
1 Corinthians 3:16,17	The body is the temple of the Holy Spirit	Pretty faces
		Traceable bodies
1 Corinthians 11:17–34	The Lord's Supper	Bread
Ephesians 6:18	Keep on praying for all the saints	Model churches
Hebrews 13:15	Sacrifice of praise	Musical praise
Revelation 19:6–9	Wedding of the Lamb	Weddings

Appendix C

Bible Topics and related prayer activities

At Mount Sinai	Exodus 19	Mountains and hills
Birth of Isaac	Genesis 21	Baby, baby
		God keeps his promises
Birth of Moses	Exodus 2:1–10	Baby, baby
Birth of Jesus Christ	Matthew 1:18–25	Baby, baby
	Luke 2:1–20	Baby, baby
Birth of Samuel	1 Samuel 1	Baby, baby
Blind Bartimaeus receives his sight	Mark 10:46–52	Glasses
Body is the temple of the Holy Spirit	1 Corinthians 3:16,17	Pretty faces
		Traceable bodies
Creation	Genesis 1–2	Creating creation
		Fun with play dough
David and Jonathan	1 Samuel 20	Friendship bracelets
David is a shepherd	1 Samuel 16:11	Baa, baa
David's psalm of thanks	1 Chronicles 16:7–36	Please and thank you
Elijah	1 Kings 17:1–6	Birds
Fall of Jericho	Joshua 6	Walls of Jericho
Fearfully and wonderfully made	Psalm 139:13,14	Pretty faces
		Mixed feelings
First-fruits and tithes	Deuteronomy 26	Play money
For God so loved the world	John 3:16–21	Hearts
For he will command his angels	Psalm 91:11	Angels
Friend loves at all times	Proverbs 17:17	Friendship bracelets
Give thanks to the Lord	Psalm 136:1–9	Please and thank you
God's covenant with Abram	Genesis 15:5,6	God keeps his promises
Hairs of your head are numbered	Luke 12:7	God loves me
I will praise you	Psalm 63:4	Musical praise
I will yet praise him	Psalm 43:5	Musical praise
Jesus anointed by a sinful woman	Luke 7:36–50	Wet feet
Jesus appears to the disciples after his resurrection	John 21:1–14	Fishing
Jesus calls Simon Peter	Luke 5:4	Fishing
Jesus calls the first disciples to be fishers of men	Mark 1:17	Fishing
Jesus feeds the five thousand	Matthew 14:13–21; Mark 6:30–34; Luke 9:10–17; John 6:1–15	Fishy fish
Jesus heals a man born blind	John 9	Glasses
Jesus is the Good Shepherd	John 10:1–18	Baa, Baa
Jesus is the light	John 1:4–5	Let light shine
Jesus prays for his disciples	John 17:6–19	Model churches
Jesus turns water into wine	John 2:1–11	Weddings
Jesus washes his disciples' feet	John 13:1–17	Wet feet
Lay down one's life for one's friends	John 15:13	Friendship bracelets
Lord is in his temple; let everyone be silent	Habakkuk 2:20	Silent prayers
Lord is my Shepherd	Psalm 23	Baa, baa
Lord's Supper	1 Corinthians 11:17–34	Bread
Mary anoints Jesus' feet	John 12:1–4	Wet feet
New commandment	John 13:34	Hearts
Parable of the sower	Matt 13:1–43	Growing seeds
Parable of the wedding banquet	Matthew 22:1–14	Weddings
Praise the Lord	Romans 15:11	Musical praise

Pray and Play

Psalm for giving thanks	Psalm 100	Praising
Ruth and Naomi	Ruth 1–4	Moving house
Sacrifice of Praise	Hebrews 13:15	Musical praise
Shout for joy... Lift up our banners	Psalm 21:5	Banners, singing and praise
Story of Joseph	Genesis 37	Coat of many colours
The Ark (God's special box)	Exodus 25:10–22	God's special box
The Festival of Shelters	Leviticus 23:33–44	Festival of Shelters
The Flood	Genesis 6:5 – 9:17	Noah's ark
		Rainbow prayers
The greatest commandment	Matthew 22:34–40	Hearts
The lamp of the body	Luke 11:33–36	Let your light shine
The Last Supper	Matthew 26:17–30	Bread
	Mark 14:12–26	
	Luke 22:7–20	
Tithe	Leviticus 27:30–33	Play money
We are God's sheep	Psalm 95:7	Baa, baa
Wedding of the Lamb	Revelation 19:6–9	Weddings

Appendix D

Subject index

Active prayers
Animal masks
Anyone thirsty?
Baa, baa
Banners, singing and praise
Games
Long-jump praying
Megaphone prayers
Mountains and hills
Moving about
Pavement prayers
Traceable bodies
Walking in the sand

Animals
Animal masks
Animals, animals, animals
Baa, baa
Birds
Creepy-crawlies
Creating creation
Finger puppets
Fishing
Fishy fish
Pet blessings
Pavement prayers
Prayer cube
Sea creatures

Bible story
Baby, baby
Coat of many colours
Creating creation
Festival of Shelters
Fishy fish
God keeps his promises
Moving house
Noah's ark
Rainbow prayers
Birds
Walls of Jericho

Bible link
Angels
Baa, baa
Banners, singing and praise
Bowling
Bread
Friendship bracelets
Fun with play dough
God loves me
God's special box

Hearts
Model churches
Mountains and hills
Musical praise
Place mats
Play money
Please and thank you
Silent prayers
Story time
Walking in the sand
Weddings
Wet feet

Christmas
Baby, baby
Pass the parcel
Toy box

Church
Circle of hands
Long-jump praying
Model churches
Pavement prayers
Stained-glass windows
Toy box
We are family

Collages
Food collage
Leaves
Paper people
Place mats
Stained-glass windows

Crafts
Button boxes
Finger puppets
Fishy fish
God's special box
Mobile families
Paper people
Prayer wheels
Rainbow prayers
Sand jars
Sea creatures
Sky
Toy box

Daily activities
ABC prayer
Badge-making
Balloons
Bedtime
Bubble, bubble, bubble
Computers
Flower decorations
Friendship bracelets

Pray and Play

Games
Glasses
Go, go, go!
Growing seeds
Megaphone prayers
Picture frames
Place mats
Please and thank you
Prayer wheels
Puzzles
Sand jars
Sea shells
Shopping
Story time
Telephones
Traceable bodies
Wakey, wakey
Watch a clock
Weather prayers

Dressing up!
Angels
Coat of many colours
God loves me
Pretty faces
Uniforms
Weather prayers

Easter
Easter eggs
Hearts

Family and home
Go, go, go!
Hearts
Lego homes
Long-jump praying
Mobile families
Pavement prayers
Pet blessings
Picture frames
Shopping

Food
Birds
Bread
Food collage
Good food
Growing seeds
Hearts
Long-jump praying
Place mats
Prayer cube

Friends
Circle of hands
Friendship bracelets
Go, go, go!

Having fun together
Long-jump praying
Making people welcome
Prayer cube

Holidays
Angels
Birthdays
Christmas
Easter eggs
Flower decorations
Hearts
Sand jars

Multi-topic prayer
ABC prayer
Long-jump praying
Pavement prayers

Obedience
Clean hands
God's special box

Ourselves
Circle of hands
Forgetting
God loves me
I can help
Long-jump praying
Mixed feelings
Moving about
Pass the parcel
Pretty faces
Shopping
Traceable bodies
Walking in the sand
Wet feet
When I hurt myself

Parties
Birthdays
Paper chains
Weddings

Praise
Banners, singing and praise
Fishy fish
Flower decorations
Musical praise

World
Go, go, go!
Good food
Long-jump praying
Moving about
Pavement prayers
Weather prayer

Glitter and Glue

101 Creative craft ideas for use with under-fives

Annette Oliver

If you have under-fives you'll know that they love making things and their work often ends up in pride of place on the wall or the fridge! Young children have an amazing capacity to learn, and using craft is a great way to help them develop co-ordination and grow in confidence. It's also a great way to begin to explore God's Word, both for the child and also their carer.

- 101 Bible-based crafts, tried and tested with the age-group
- Step-by-step guides to preparation and materials
- Comprehensive introduction with tips on different craft techniques
- Find your way around easily with a Bible and theme index
- All templates fully photocopiable!

ISBN 1 85999 599 3   A4, 96pp

For playgroups...
For carer and toddler groups...
For church children's groups

Have you enjoyed this book?

Then take a look at the other Big Books in the *Tiddlywinks* range. Why not try them all?

Tiddlywinks Big Books are designed for use in any pre-school setting. The multi-purpose outlines are packed full of play, prayers, crafts, stories and rhymes; simply pick and mix ideas to meet the particular needs of your group. You'll find plenty of practical advice on setting up and running a pre-school group, plus ideas in every session to help you include adult carers. The children will love the illustrated activity pages.
A4, 96pp, £8.99 each

You can order these or any other *Tiddlywinks* resources from:

- Your local Christian bookstore
- Scripture Union Mail Order: Telephone 01908 856006
- Online: log on to **www.scriptureunion.org.uk/publishing** to order securely from our online bookshop

Tiddlywinks
The flexible resource for pre-school children and carers

Coming soon!
Even more books and an exciting range of Tiddlywinks merchandise...